A FORGIVING WIND

Fred Powledge

A
FORGIVING
WIND
On Becoming a Sailor

⊿⊿⊿

Sierra Club Books   San Francisco

The Sierra Club, founded in 1892 by John Muir, has devoted itself
to the study and protection of the earth's scenic and ecological resources—
mountains, wetlands, woodlands, wild shores and rivers, deserts and plains.
The publishing program of the Sierra Club offers books to the public as a
nonprofit educational service in the hope that they may enlarge the
public's understanding of the Club's basic concerns. The point of view
expressed in each book, however, does not necessarily represent that of the Club.
The Sierra Club has some fifty chapters coast to coast, in Canada, Hawaii, and
Alaska.
For information about how you may participate in its programs to
preserve wilderness and the quality of life, please address inquiries to:
Sierra Club, 530 Bush Street, San Francisco, CA 94108.

Library of Congress Cataloging in Publication Data
Powledge, Fred
A forgiving wind.
Bibliography: p. 205
Includes index.
1. Seamanship.   2. Sailing.   I. Title.
GV777.5.P68   1983   623.88   82-16867

ISBN 0-87156-330-4

Jacket design by Muriel Nasser
Book design by Abigail Johnston
Illustrations by Gordon J. Morrison

Printed in the United States of America

10 9 8 7 6 5 4 3 2 1

For Patrick William Powledge,

who sails a sea I do not know

Acknowledgments

For all their help and support, and for literally making the thoughts behind this book possible, I am deeply grateful to Andrew Denmark, Mary Denmark, Naomi Morrison, A.S.L. Peaslee, Tabitha M. Powledge, and Steve Rubin.

Contents

A FORGIVING WIND

Introduction

This is not a book about how to sail. There are dozens of those books, and I think I can say with some confidence that all of them were written by people who are far more competent sailors than I. Besides, a book can teach you only so much about how to sail. As with cross-country skiing, backpacking, canoeing, and no doubt a hundred other activities, the written word (or, for that matter, the filmed image) can convey only some of the things that an interested novice requires in order to get started, or that an energetic student needs to improve and build on what he or she already knows.

The time comes quickly in sailing, as it does in those other sports and avocations, when what is to be learned can be learned best in person, up close, on the water and in the wind. (Books are very good, however, in helping you along the way to that wonderful moment, and at the end of this book there is a list, called "Sources," of those publications that have been most helpful to me.)

This *is* a book about becoming a sailor. As such, it can only be a highly personal and personalized account. There are multitudinous dangers in such an accounting. It is terribly easy, for example, for the chronicler to assume incorrectly that the experiences, fantasies, trials and (most inevitably) errors that went into *his* learning are (or worse, have to be) the same for everyone else. I have tried to avoid this trap, and if I have failed to avoid it completely, I apologize at the outset. One of the many fine things that my own, still-evolving experience with sailing has taught me is that, while unrestricted egocentricity may work like a charm for tennis stars, baseball managers, television celebrities, and even—temporarily, at least—some America's Cup contenders, generally speaking it does not work well at all for ordinary sailors. If you become too self-centered in a sailboat, if you are certain that you are right, you will be very susceptible to running aground and to heading toward buoys that are not the ones you thought they were.

Here, as in most everything else, is an endless parade of tradeoffs: You've got to be *some* sure of yourself or you'll never be able to screw up the courage to get away from the dock. You've got to exude *some* audacious self-confidence because there is usually someone else in the boat who is afraid it's going to turn over, or sink, or meet with some other horrible fate, and it is one of your jobs to convince this person (and occasionally yourself as well) of the contrary.

Another danger has to do with a component of sailing that the sailor quickly recognizes as a very important one, and that I will explore more thoroughly later on. That is the fact that sailing and sailors are always functioning on some sort of moving continuum of experience and competence. One's ability to sail "properly," whatever that is (it can mean something as seemingly complicated as winning a single-handed around-the-world race and it can mean something as seemingly simple as bringing the boat into a peaceful conjunction with the dock without destroying either structure), is always changing—one hopes for the better. What is very complicated at one moment may be old hat a few days or weeks later, after you've gained a little experience. The danger with this is that someone who is at Point C or D on that continuum, and who presumes to write a book or otherwise pass along information on the subject, is very likely to get a lot of horse laughs from those who are at Points J, K, and beyond. The only defense here is to remind the folks at Point J or K that there is someone *else* at Point M or N who knows even more than they do, and to ask for leniency.

Just as it is easy to forget that all sailors, and people who are interested in becoming sailors, function at wildly differing and constantly changing levels of ability, it is easy to slip into the assumption that everyone else who sails feels the same way as you do about sailing. This can be a real shocker if you haven't thought about it. It can be like going to a dinner party and *assuming* that everyone else at the table shares your political beliefs, and then discovering that they emphatically don't. The attitudes sailors bring to sailing are about as diverse as the variations the manufacturers have made on the design of the classic cruising sloop. Some people love sailing because they love racing. Others love it because it is such a profoundly *slow* way to get from one place to another—so slow, in comparison with the rest of modern life, as to represent a vigorous nose-thumb at that life.

Some love it because it serves as a conduit to nature, in much the same way that backpacking, day-hiking, and cross-country skiing function as devices by which a human not only can have fun, but also may re-connect her- or himself to the natural forces that make life possible on Earth.

A Forgiving Wind

Some people love sailing because it brings them solitude. (I remember especially George, separated from his wife and family and most of the other people in the world, who lived aboard his boat in the salty waters of eastern North Carolina and who, each evening after a day of repairing other people's Mercedes-Benzes, would scrub his hands clean and sail all night with running lights off, like some modern-day Flying Dutchman, searching while others slept for something that he was not himself able to define very clearly.) Some love it because it brings them the very opposite of solitude. (In the same waters George cruised, there was a boat that from time to time went out loaded with men who looked like middle-aged L.A. movie execs and women who looked like younger-aged L.A. movie hopefuls, although it was the wrong coast for this, and that would return and disgorge dozens of wine and liquor bottles and crinkled aluminum-foil potato-chip-dip containers.) Some want gregariousness without the muss and fuss of heeling over, hoisting sails, and tending the tiller. We have all seen those people, spending entirely contented weekends with their boats tied securely to the dock, the bottoms of their Topsiders barely dulled, the slumber of the little alligators on their polo shirts hardly disturbed.

Some are excited by the prospect, often not articulated but always present, of danger. (The very act of putting a boat into the water and then operating it in such a way that it tilts far over on its side is a form of danger-courting, even if you *do* know all about its center of gravity.) And some people love sailing for reasons that they do not understand, cannot articulate, and are quite perplexed about, but hope someday to be able to explain, both to their friends who inquire politely and to themselves.

When I began sailing, just a few years ago, I naturally asked myself what I liked about it. My curiosity was made sharper by the fact that for most of my life (as I shall explain

Introduction

shortly) I had had a distinct dislike for the sport, a dislike deeply rooted in total ignorance about sailing.

My immediate reply to my self-inquiry was the "sailing-is-a-conduit-to-nature" one; that taking off in a boat that is powered only by the wind is in many ways similar to hiking along the crest of the Blue Ridge or skiing down some logging road in Vermont, two other avocations in which I delight and which I have always wished I had more time for. But as I do more sailing, and as my feelings for the sport become deeper and broader, I realize that I am drawn to it for *all* the reasons mentioned above, as well as a few others that are not listed. At first, for example, I scoffed at racing and at sailors who ate, slept, and breathed racing; but one time I was sailing in a nice breeze on a lake in Michigan and noticed another boat, similar in size to mine, on the same tack and not far away, and I waved at the skipper and the skipper waved back at me and then we both hauled in our jib sheets and started paying more attention to what we were doing, and I gradually realized that we were *racing*—and, astoundingly, that I was enjoying it. At dinner that night I was surprised to hear myself uttering something about "beating the stuffing" out of the gentleman.

Sailing also has become for me a means of achieving solitude as well as a way to have fun with good friends. I like a bit of danger a bit of the time, and I like the idea of going slowly in a fast-moving world. Sailing has done other things to and for me: It has made me aware, in a way that city-dwellers often are not, of the importance and beauty of weather, and I have become more interested in reading the clouds and winds and in trying to predict what's on the way. It has made me appreciate, in a way that city-dwellers often are simply incapable of appreciating, the night-time sky.

Sailing has given me other bonuses that I never would have anticipated. For one, I find myself in what the rest of the world seems to refer to, and what I myself thought of, until I got there, as "middle age." Sailing, I realize with great joy, is something—is perhaps one of the few things in our youth-crazed culture—that you get better at as you get older. Another unanticipated dividend comes from my growing interest in navigation and would probably bowl over an entire series of dedicated but frustrated elementary and high school teachers in the public school system of Raleigh, North Carolina, if they were informed of it now: I have learned to love mathematics, and for a very simple reason. For the first time in my life, I have found the science of numbers and triangles and sines and cosines to be *useful* to me.

And so I must conclude that I love sailing because it gives me things that make me feel good: things that are worthy and lasting and that both stretch my brain and please my eye; that demand from me the skills that I have learned; that reward me for doing the right things; that (more often than not, at least) are forgiving in their punishment when I do something wrong. Paradoxically—for sailing really must be done according to a large number of rules and constraints—sailing gives me a great deal of freedom. Finally, when things are going well and even sometimes when they aren't, sailing gives me a reminder of the immortality that we all used to think we had, back when we were kids.

Even though it is dangerous to assume that sailing means the same things to all people, and even though I am trying to avoid that pitfall in this book, I suspect that those last-mentioned qualities come pretty close to being universal ones. When you learn to sail, you learn a good deal about yourself. And you become a little more free.

1

HOW IT
HAPPENS

CHAPTER ONE

First, How It Didn't Happen

For me, the fascination with becoming a sailor occurred well after my fortieth year, and it occurred after a lifetime of very un-sailor-like behavior and feelings.

It would be incorrect to say that I hated sailing during all those years when I was growing up. You need to *know* something about something in order to *hate* it, and I knew very little about anything that was tinged with exoticism, as was sailing at that time and place. I lived in Raleigh, North Carolina, which was the state capital but which in those days had only about sixty thousand residents and managed very skillfully to repel any overtures of cosmopolitanism that the rest of the world might make. My first impressions of Chinese and Italian foods, for example, were of two gelatinous goops, one of them vaguely yellow and called "chop suey" and the other a reddish-brown mass that quickly underwent meltdown and changed into heartburn. (Fortunately, I have undertaken a course of gastronomic therapy since then.) My first impressions of live music, beyond that offered by church choirs, did not occur until I got into college. I had fine and memorable schoolteachers, but the public school administration was terrified of controversy in those pre-McCarthy years, so horizons were kept as close to home as possible. The town's most rabid personality was a right-wing radio commentator who was *so* right-wing that the left-wingers used to listen to him to confirm their prejudices against right-wingers. His name was Jesse Helms.

Raleigh was landlocked, being a hundred or so miles removed from the Atlantic and the delicious system of sounds and bays that blesses the North Carolina coast. The water of my youth was muddy, sewery Crabtree Creek, which my cousin David and I used to explore on foot and in homemade rafts. But that was exploring the *jungle* alongside the creek (we were influenced, as was everyone at that time, by World War II, particularly by the war in the Pacific); that was not exploring *water*. I remained ignorant of sailing.

But I managed nevertheless to hold sailing in very low esteem because of the company it kept. The word, among my friends and everyone's parents in that lower-middle-class segment of society of which we were members, was that the people who went sailing were the same people who played golf and tennis and who belonged to the Country Club. The rich. It was quite easy to think of people who sailed as people who wore dumb-looking caps and ascots and monocles and who said things like "Pip, pip, old boy" and referred to what they were doing as "Yachting." (To say it correctly, you must propel the first syllable with extreme gentleness from the very roof of your mouth, which you hold open in an exaggerated manner, as if you were trying to avoid damaging the word.) My friends and I reserved for sailing people the same sort of derision we might heap now on British gentlemen who write letters to *The Times* complaining about the servant problem.

This mindless prejudice was not based strictly on class jealousy, although that certainly helped. It was reinforced by experience, as well. For one thing, my home, which had been built on what was one of the outskirts of Raleigh, quickly got surrounded by suburbia, which underwent almost geometrical expansion throughout the nation in the postwar years. The particular side of town we lived on happened to be the one the better-off people chose for their homes. (Each American city now has one or more "good" and one or more "bad" sides, and most of them were established in the postwar years. They are instantly recognizable by the sorts of shopping centers and fast-food joints that hunker down among, and sometimes clearly dominate, them. These strange citadels of pavement and Muzak and plastic philodendrons are better indicators of the surrounding area's socioeconomic level than the most recent census data.) Such an abundance of better-off people chose our side of town, in fact, that they had to have a country club there.

When I was a kid I hung around the club a bit, doing odd jobs and caddying for the golfers, and avoiding no opportunities to glimpse the wealthy of Raleigh at play and drink. I found that some of them (particularly the ones who had had money for a long time, like the older physicians) were perfectly nice, but that many of the others who had lately clawed their way into the Forties definition of "society" were stuffy, inconsiderate, snobbish, somewhat obnoxious people who knew a lot less than they let on and who seemed to drink a lot. (That last may not have been entirely their fault. Liquor-by-the-drink was illegal in North Carolina then, and this meant that when people consumed alcohol they tended to consume it furtively, guiltily, and to excess. It also meant that private clubs were essential to socializing, so a country club's bar could be as important an attraction for some people as its golf course.)

A Forgiving Wind

The impression I had of rich people was further engraved on my mind when I took over a newspaper route, delivering *The Raleigh Times* in the late afternoon to several dozen families near my home. Because the neighborhood was undergoing a metamorphosis from outskirt to fashionable suburbia, several of the original outskirt people had not yet had their property charmed away from them or their leases jerked out from under them, and these people turned out, as they almost always do, to be poor whites and blacks. So my route comprised both poor and wealthy, black and white, day-laborer and thoracic surgeon, along with a lot of post-war *nouveaux riches* to fill in the gaps. I soon found that it was the desperately poor families who lived in the unpainted wood-and-tarpaper shacks at the foot of Saint Mary's Street (shacks owned by a wealthy pillar of local society) who paid their bills promptly and even cheerfully once a week. They often invited me in to have a glass of iced tea with them on especially hot Fridays, my collection days. The huge, expensive homes up the hill, the ones owned by the dentist, the realtor, and the fellow who had the town's leading auto dealership, contained the worst deadbeats on the route. It was always, "The doctor's at the hospital today; we'll pay you next week." It was *that* sort of people with whom I learned, early in my life, to associate such exotic pastimes as golf, tennis, skiing, sailing—and, of course, the money with which those interests could be pursued.

I have gone on at such great length about this because I know that I was not alone in developing such prejudices. The perceived association between sailing and wealth and snootiness has been a strong one, and it persists even to this day. There are a lot of people on dry land right now who could be getting tremendous enjoyment out of sailing, but who are restrained by their refusal to mispronounce "Yachting."

△ △ △

A number of things happened, as the years passed, to change all my feelings. One of them was that I got older and a little smarter and met a lot more different human beings and became reluctant to classify people into majestically sweeping stereotypes. Other occurrences were perhaps more basic to the fabric of society as a whole.

World War II ended. It is difficult, even now with a great deal of hindsight, to comprehend all the changes that were brought to American life as a result of that. In a transition that I remember as all-of-a-sudden, but that could only have been a gradual chain of events, people became mobile. As if awakening from a long, hard winter of enforced isolation, we stretched our legs and hurried off to see the things we'd been denied for so long. The rationing of gasoline and rubber tires ended, and it was possible to think of a trip in the family automobile as fun, rather than a potentially unpatriotic act. The machinery that had been building aircraft carriers and dive-bombers switched over to manufacturing rowboats and Studebakers with little propellers on their noses. (That same machinery supported the people on my newspaper route who sold and repaired the new cars and who slipped so easily into the role of *nouveau riche* deadbeat.)

Surviving soldiers, sailors, pilots, and Marines came home, and people started building families. Human settlement pushed past municipal outskirts like a giant game of leapfrog, and yesterday's suburbia quickly became part of the city itself (and, in one of the better examples of inadvertent social justice, soon would find itself headed for "inner city" status). Existing roads and highways were inadequate to splice all these split-level developments to the urban centers and to each other, so a phony excuse was dreamed up to build a nationwide network of high-speed roadways, one benefit of which would be to carry the better-off from their homes to their jobs, often over the very heads of the less-well-off. (The excuse was that the Interstate Highway System, with its numerous Business Loops and Perimeter Roads, was essential for the civil defense of the nation—it would enable the residents of cities to be evacuated to the bucolic and relatively safe countryside when "the Communists" started raining down their Cold War rockets.)

The work-week got shorter. My father, a state employee who had put in five and one-half days a week, or more, all his life, went to a five-day schedule and moaned about how he was somehow cheating the taxpayers. Eventually he overcame that guilt, but he continued to put on a suit and tie on Saturday mornings. Elsewhere, work-weeks that had been forty or forty-eight hours shrunk to thirty-six or even thirty. People discovered that they had space in which to park more than their station wagon out there in their suburban driveways—there was room for a boat, too—and they had time on their hands that they hadn't had before, and they now had highways that would take them places quickly and in relative safety. It therefore became practically mandatory that the government build them lots of places they could visit in order to have their "recreational experiences."

An obvious solution to this dilemma was to create large bodies of water. This would benefit every segment of society, with the exceptions of the families who would be dispossessed of their land, and of the natural world, which would be forever scarred by the giant construction projects. But we were not talking much about the environment in those days, and the environment had not yet started talking so clearly to us.

First, How It Didn't Happen

Who would benefit from the construction of large water projects? The builders, the ones who ran the bulldozers and cement mixers; the land speculators, who could count on the federal government's assistance (to the point of exercising its right of eminent domain on their behalf) in taking land from farmers and reselling it, at shockingly inflated prices now that it was "prime lakefront property," to marina operators, second-home buyers, motel chains, and industrialists; the barge companies, in those cases involving navigable waterways (of which there were many in the Tennessee Valley Authority projects); and the government building agencies, chief among them the Corps of Engineers and TVA, which used water projects as handy devices for staying robustly alive in the bureaucratic thickets. And, of course, the ordinary post-war American, the person with a shorter work-week, bigger driveway, fatter paycheck, and greater mobility. The reservoirs and hydro projects were billed universally as water *recreation* projects, as well, because that helped the builders prove that the benefits of a given project would outweigh its costs. Furthermore, who could possibly be against *recreation*? The purported recreational value of a water project helped dignify it, helped make it economically and philosophically respectable, just as the Interstate Highway scheme had been justified by that fantasy about millions of Americans calmly evacuating their home towns via I-95 or Business Loop 80 while the Russians dropped their missiles on silent, deserted parking garages and F. W. Woolworth stores.

The popularity of water recreation got another boost from the development and widespread use of fiber glass as a boat-building material. It was relatively lightweight and relatively inexpensive, and it did not require the almost continuous attention and maintenance that wood demanded. A lot of ordinary people who did not *ever* go

"Yachting" got themselves boats and hauled them "up to the lake" on weekends. Most of these boats were designed to be driven strictly by a mixture of petroleum and beer, and most of those that were not used for trying to catch fish were employed in noisily dragging people on skis around the lake. But the designers and manufacturers of sailboats learned about fiber glass, too, and they started using the material. Fiber glass sloops started appearing in coastal waters, and on the lakes it became not unusual to see the tiny, beautiful sail of a lone Sunfish, venturing courageously out among the bass boats and skihogs.

Little if any official thought was given, of course, to the idea of *not* producing highly developed sources of "recreational experiences"—to using our national talents instead for protecting more wilderness areas or saving more of the coastline from degradation, or to just pointing at the mountains and saying, "See, aren't they beautiful? Why don't you go walking there?" We had been living like primitives all during the war years, and now it was time for some luxury. We started riding a crest of affluence that would last into the Seventies; our future, even the future of our spare time and recreation, would be one, we thought, in which nature was shaped to *our* needs, for *our* comfort. Mention "backpacking" in those days and you were likely to conjure up visions of someone disappearing into the woods loaded down with heavy, inefficient Army surplus pack and puptent, and who wanted *that*? (Lots of folks did, as it turned out, but the nation didn't notice them until it discovered down and ripstop nylon and mountain boots some years later.)

There were other changes that occurred in the postwar period that had, in circuitious ways, something to do with my and others' feelings about sailing and sailboats. The nation got excited about education, and it got particularly excited about making sure that everyone who wanted one had a *college* education. Since the big, established institutions weren't about to change their rules to allow anyone in who wanted to come in, new colleges were brought to the people. Teachers' colleges and community institutions became part of the state university systems. The academic world, formerly restricted to a few campuses and the larger cities, invaded every medium-sized city in the nation, along with many smaller ones. Invasions and subsequent occupations have classically served as efficient, if drastic, ways of spreading ideas and attitudes. The decentralization of higher education helped to disseminate attitudes about foods, religions, economic philosophy, and recreation in places that had been quite provincial. Chinese and Italian restaurants opened up that served something other than gelatinous goop, and canoes and sailboats started showing up on TVA lakes that had held nothing but motorboats.

Simultaneously (all these events, in fact, seemed simultaneous), we were developing from a society in which owing money was considered an early sign of moral failure into one in which almost everything we bought was obtained on credit. That meant that a lot of people who wanted to own boats, but who couldn't because they cost too much, could now buy boats, just as they had bought automobiles and houses. There was the germ, and then the evolution, and finally the self-destructive fruition of the notion that if you can't afford something you just go into debt to get it, for tomorrow not only you may die but also the thing you want may cost twice as much as it costs today. And—of great importance—there was the realization by many of those who *had* borrowed the money and bought the boat that they were broke all the time, and their subsequent discovery that they could amortize the cost by renting the boat out to someone else when they weren't using it.

This last event made it possible for people like me, who

probably will never be able to own a sailboat, to go sailing from time to time and to spend no more on it than my family would spend on a moderately-priced vacation, if such a thing still exists.

By the late Seventies, then, sailing had come an enormous distance from the rich-man's-and-snob's sport that I, as a youth, had perceived it as being. But little of this had had any influence on me and on my attitude toward sailing, and there the matter would have stayed if it hadn't been for a couple of pleasant accidents. If they hadn't occurred, I would have continued to wallow in my ignorance and to get a lot less out of life. Every time I passed a sailboat marina, if I glanced that way at all, I would have seen a confusing tangle of masts, cross-arms, booms, cables, and wires, and I probably would have thought that it sure looked like a lot of work. And if I had done much thinking about what I saw, I would have noted the fact that even though it was a fine summer (or spring, or fall) weekend, the great majority of the sailboats were tied up at the dock, with no sign that their owners were coming to take them on outings. And so it would have been reasonable for me to speculate that sailing wasn't really all that much fun, or else why weren't these boats out there cutting through the water?

And I would have passed on to other, and presumably more important, things, and sailing never would have entered my life. But then came the pleasant accidents. They occurred when I bumped into three people who frequented two bodies of water almost a thousand miles apart—Andy and Mary Denmark in Oriental, North Carolina, and Strat Peaslee in Lake Walloon, Michigan.

CHAPTER TWO

Oriental

I had been to Oriental many years before, and the place had lodged in my memory beside Savannah and the North and South Carolina Beauforts as an attractive, comfortable example of people's attempts at living by the sea. I was a child when I visited Oriental; I'd gone to a YMCA summer camp a few miles farther up the Neuse River, and one day we went down to Oriental—could it be that we *sailed* down there in the camp's Lightnings and Comets?—and watched the shrimpers drop their catches at the dock in the well-protected town harbor. The wives and children of the men who had caught the shrimp came down to the combination dock–warehouse and helped with the unloading. The black families of Oriental came down and started processing the shrimp—cleaning them, peeling them, packing them for shipment by trucks to inland towns. There was not much freezing: Seafood was as likely then to be fresh as today it is to be frozen. Our counselor bought some shrimp off one of the boats, and I remember that it cost sixty cents a pound, heads on and unpeeled.

Although Oriental had stuck in my memory—perhaps as much as anything else because of its name, which had been borrowed by the townsfolk from the nameplate of a wrecked freighter, and because of my recollection of those shrimp—it had stuck there behind a lot of other memories until Blaine Liner mentioned it in the summer of 1977. I was interviewing Liner, the director of the Southern Growth Policies Board, for a newspaper series and book I was writing on the modern South. One of my consuming interests while I was doing that research, and since then as well, was the ways in which the region was coping with its economic growth. Would my native land, which was enjoying a great deal of popularity compliments of the "Sunbelt" phenomenon, remember to protect the aspect of itself that made it so attractive in the first place—its environment?

There was someone in Oriental, said Liner, who was dealing with that question at first hand. The fellow had been trained and employed in the most modern sorts of technological thinking and systems analysis, but he had dropped out of that promising career to open up a sailboat marina on the North Carolina coast. The gentleman had to confront all sorts of basic questions because, while sailing in its purest form disturbs nature amazingly little, building a sailboat marina means disrupting the environment quite a bit: there is dredging to be done, and construction to be started, wells to be dug, sewage to be disposed of.

It was late spring. I could use a trip to the coast. Who was this fellow? Liner said his name was Andy Denmark.

Andy Denmark, known then as "Drew," had been a kid in my neighborhood at the time when I was a kid in my neighborhood. We had occasionally played together, and had frequently seen each other on the sidewalks and playgrounds, although we hadn't been close friends because

Drew was a couple of years younger than I, and in child-
hood a couple of years makes a lot of difference. After my
talk with Blaine Liner I called Denmark in Oriental—his
marina was named "Sailcraft"—and he said he remembered
me with about the same intensity that I remembered him.
Sure, he said, he'd like very much to talk about the future of
the coast. Come on down any time.

△△△

It was amazing, but Oriental had hardly changed. Surely
the town was no larger than I had remembered it, although
when I looked closer I could see a few houses that obviously
had been built recently. The harbor was the same, the
commercial docks were the same, and I was pretty sure the
names of the seafood companies and of some of their trawl-
ers were the same. The ancient live oaks still stood along
the streets, in some cases rudely heaving sidewalks out of
the way and forcing a detour around their massive, twisting
roots. The wonderful old frame houses, painted white and
obviously well-maintained, still kept watch along the shore.
Traffic, be it foot or bicycle or even automobile, moved
extremely slowly through the town. And, I noticed with
sadness, there were still clear boundaries between the ter-
ritories occupied by black people and those occupied by
white people. Oriental's population was maybe three
hundred and fifty, and her median age must have been
considerably higher than the nation's as a whole. Certainly
the levels of comfort and beauty were higher.

Oriental is neither a river town nor a coastal port, but
rather a combination of both that is not at all unusual in
eastern North Carolina. The coastal region of the state is
drained by a number of rivers, the greatest of which—the
Chowan, the Pamlico, and the Neuse—empty into two

large sounds. Eastward of the sounds (the Albemarle, which receives the waters of the Chowan and other rivers, and the Pamlico, which is fed by the Pamlico and Neuse Rivers) are the famed Outer Banks, which are thin strips of dunes, marsh, and beach. Beyond the Banks, and on occasion washing over them, is the Atlantic Ocean.

The rivers open their mouths wide as they flow into the sounds, and it is impossible to identify the exact, or even approximate, point at which their water stops being river and starts being sound. The federal government, of course, feels a compunction to designate such a point even if one does not exist, and so the "Neuse River Entrance" has been duly established, engraved on nautical charts, and graced with a twenty-five-foot-tall light that flashes, once each six seconds, for the benefit of those who might otherwise have missed the elusive moment of demarcation.

One of the joys of Oriental, and of much of coastal North Carolina, is that the region is off the beaten track. The abundance of water has made it difficult for the bridge- and dam-builders to do their usual things here, and so the harmful development that characterizes so much of the Atlantic seaboard has been retarded. Also, much of the coastal environment is technically part of the Great Dismal Swamp, and fortunately the sort of people who are in the market for condominiums and second homes are leery about places that have "swamp" in their names. Oriental, and the dozens of towns like it along the coast, are not antiques, restored little fragments of Charleston floating in formaldehyde, but rather working communities, and that makes them all the more pleasing. They have not been boutiqued to death. I have not yet seen a tee shirt that celebrates the wonders of Oriental, North Carolina, and if I ever do, I shall be sad indeed.

A few things had changed by the time I returned in the late Seventies, of course. On the road into town there was a small, tasteful billboard announcing the creation of a second-home-type development nearby, but that was the only mention I heard of it. And there were sailboat marinas, at least three of them, in Oriental that hadn't been there before. The marinas were situated on Whittaker Creek, a narrow tidal body that opens into the Neuse, which when it passes Oriental is about three nautical miles wide. Sailcraft was one of the marinas on Whittaker Creek.

I met Andy and his wife, Mary (they since have parted), and their curly-headed daughter, Melissa, and we talked about the old days in the neighborhood. It was obvious that the slight difference in our ages, as important as it may have been back then, made no difference now. Andy had grown to six feet, four inches, with a full head of blond hair, and his rugged features reflected the wind and sun well. I could understand why he might have grown tired of a job that required him to sit indoors all day with a mathematical calculator in his hand. Mary was tanned and healthy-looking, too, with curly red hair and a very quick wit. Together, with occasional interruptions brought on by the business of running a marina, we talked about the coast and why they had come there and what they hoped to accomplish. One thing they wanted to do that they hadn't done enough of, they said, was sailing. Andy pointed out their thirty-foot C&C sloop, *Odyssey*, at the dock, and he complained about how operating the marina left them little time to get out on the water themselves.

I was impressed by the informality and lack of pretense of the place and of the people who ran and frequented it. Nobody spoke of "Yachting." Strangers said "Hello," and asked questions like "What brings you here?"

Once, during a break in our interviewing, I wandered along the dock alone and watched a middle-aged man arrive in his car, go aboard his boat, ready his sails for hoisting, and head slowly under engine power out of the channel toward the river and sound. I wondered how difficult it was to direct the boat away from the dock—he had to back his out into Whittaker Creek, where a fairly strong current struck him from the side until he got his boat straightened out. But the man knew what he was doing. He had figured the current into his calculations, and he timed his turns so that the current actually helped him. He made the maneuver look easy. When he was properly in the channel and headed for the large green daymarker at the end of the creek, he looked back toward the dock, saw me watching, and waved. I waved back. You could not see the Neuse from the marina, and I wondered where the boat was going and what it would look like on the big body of water.

Noon came and all of us—the Denmarks, I, and everyone who worked at the marina or who happened to be there tending his boat—piled into a couple of cars and drove the mile or so to the Oriental Marina, across the commercial harbor from the seafood docks, which had a fine restaurant. We gorged ourselves on sandwiches, shrimp, and salad, and after Andy finished up what anybody else couldn't eat we returned to Sailcraft.

By late afternoon I had asked all my questions, and Andy asked me what my plans were. I could stay at a motel, I said, or I could continue on down the coast toward my next interview. Nonsense, said Andy. "You'll stay here, if you want to. On *Odyssey*."

I was hesitant at first, although the idea instantly intrigued me. I have gotten pretty stuck in my ways in recent years. I find, for instance, that not only must I have a cup of coffee upon awakening, but that it must be brewed to my precise specifications; and I find that I really must have some privacy during part of my day. The idea of sleeping on someone's boat was an extraordinary one for someone who is stuck in his ways, and all the more so if it's done on the spur of the moment. Of course, I agreed. I may be stuck in my ways, but I also fancy myself a person who's eager to experiment.

I woke at three in the morning, as I always do when I'm in a strange place. It took a moment for me to remember where I was, and then I became aware of a number of things that were completely foreign to my experience. There were the smells of teak and fiber glass, and there was the realization that I was longer than the bunk I was sleeping on and that there was no space, as there is at home, for my feet to hang over the end. There was the shape of the cabin, which was outlined in the soft light of the dock lamps—a shape that held me in, constrained me in its gentle, protective oval as no room in a house or motel could, or even as the tiny protected space of a backpacking tent would. But most of all, I was aware of the soft rocking motion of *Odyssey*. No other boats were passing; the motion came from the breeze and from the tidal current as it entered Whittaker Creek. It was restful, I decided once I had its rhythms figured out, and I fell asleep again.

When I woke it was a crisp, blue day, almost like early fall in the Northeast, and there was a nice breeze. I felt wonderful. I climbed out onto the dock (not expertly; the tide had placed deck and dock at different levels now, and I couldn't figure out how to get gracefully over or through the lifelines). I walked barefoot along the thick wooden planks, inspecting the other sailboats. Somehow they looked a little less foreign to me, their rigging a little less complex. Was it possible that mere proximity to sailboats made them more understandable?

As I walked, I could still feel the rocking sensation, even though the dock was solidly implanted in the ground. What a curious thing, I thought; I wonder if the feeling will go away. I wasn't sure I *wanted* it to disappear; it felt almost pleasant—or maybe I enjoyed it because it was a certification that I had slept aboard a sailboat. It was a fine day to be alive, I thought; I wonder if I would also enjoy actually sailing in one of the things.

"How'd you like to go out in a sailboat?" asked Mary. The answer was written all over my face.

Mary had her own boat, a Cape Dory Typhoon, which at eighteen feet is near the smaller limits of comfort and safety for a sailboat on marginally protected salt water. (Having said that, I must quickly back away from it. There *are* no such limits on what should sail where, as has been proven by the people who have journeyed alone across oceans in boats not much bigger than walnut shells. Robert Manry, for example, a newspaper copyeditor from Cleveland, sailed from Falmouth, Massachusetts, to Falmouth, England, in seventy-eight days in a thirteen-foot, mostly homemade, wooden boat named *Tinkerbelle*.) The Typhoon has a small cabin, barely big enough for an adult to crawl into, and it is just the right size for exploring the shallower reaches of coastal North Carolina.

"Do you know the buoyage system?" asked Mary as we started down the channel. She had cranked a tiny outboard and was using the tiller to guide us toward the green beacon that rose out of the water on a thick piling. The sails were down; the jib was folded in the cabin and the main was neatly bundled along the boom.

"You want to keep the greens on your right when you're going out into the deeper water, and the reds on your left. When you see one that's black, that's the same as a green. And they come in all shapes and sizes. The important thing's the color. See the one ahead of us? The green square? We pass that one on our right, then make a sharp turn to the right, and we'll see more markers, some red and some green. They mark the channel out into the river itself, into the deep water. On the way back it's just the reverse. Reds on your right, greens or blacks on your left. Most people remember it by 'Red right returning.'"

"Red right returning," I said, fairly certain that it wouldn't stick with me. But it has.

We made a right-hand turn to follow the creek out into the river. The outboard made a racket. As the stream widened and we slowly pulled away from the protection of land and trees, the wind increased and I could feel our gentle rocking motion change as the placid water turned into small waves. Out ahead, in the river, the water looked busier still (the word in my mind then was "rougher," not "busier"), and I thought I could even see a whitecap or two. Mary had been reading my mind. "Looks like a fine day for sailing," she said. She knew that I lacked any standard, any frame of reference in which to judge the wind and waves. Eventually I learned that the construction of just such a frame of reference through experience is one of the most important steps in becoming a sailor. For the moment it helped a great deal to know that someone who *did* know what she was doing, and whom I trusted, thought that the conditions were ideal for sailing.

On the way out the channel, Mary explained that many of Sailcraft's customers were relatively new to sailing and that almost invariably, when a sailboat was owned by a husband and wife, it was the husband who initially had become interested in the sport, who had read up on it and learned how to do it, who had taken lessons if necessary, and who had been the prime mover in the selection and purchase of the boat.

"The woman almost always sort of tags along behind," said Mary. "She may be very interested, but she's really lacking in a lot of information about how it all works, and so she tends to stay behind. She gets consulted about the 'feminine' things like the layout of the cabin, and the galley, and the head, but that's about all. It's pretty archaic, really. It's also very frustrating, and a lot of the wives have said something about it to me. So I started doing a kind of informal sailing-lesson thing with them."

I asked Mary what it consisted of.

"Just what we're doing here today," she replied.

Mary turned the tiny engine down to very slow and handed me the tiller. "Here," she said. "Try to keep it pointed directly into the wind, and I'm going to start putting up the sails." Before I could advise her that I wasn't too sure about where "directly into the wind" was, she had gone to the mast and started hoisting the mainsail. It rose easily along its track. Then Mary scrambled along the narrow side deck up to the bow of the boat. She had a small sail, folded into a neat package, in one hand, and I noticed that even as she was moving or fastening the sail on, she managed quite expertly to keep a hand or the crook of an arm on something secure—one of the cables that came down from the mast, the lifeline, a stanchion. I wondered how difficult it would be to do that when the boat was rocking in strong wind and waves. While I wondered I forgot about the tiller, and Mary yelled at me, "Into the wind!" I overcompensated, and we swung off into the other direction. Gradually I got the Typhoon's nose pointed again roughly in the direction from which the wind was coming. It was easy to see that everything calmed down considerably when the nose of the boat pointed straight at the wind, cutting it like a sharp knife so that half of the wind (if that can be imagined) ran down one side of the boat and half down the other.

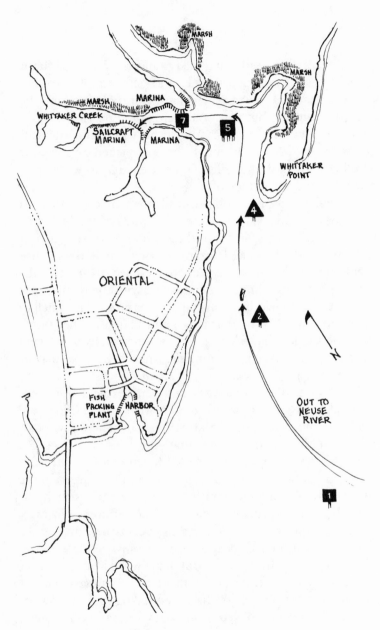

Oriental and environs

A Forgiving Wind

Mary had the sails up quickly, and she returned to the cockpit, sat down opposite me, and gently took the tiller from my hand. We were still pointing at the wind, and the sails did nothing but flap. We were going nowhere. Mary eased us away from directly into the wind, and the sails immediately filled with air and the boat picked up speed. It also heeled over a little, although not enough to worry me. Mary turned the engine off.

I will always remember the silence that came then. It was not *truly* silent; there were the sounds of the breeze in the sails and the rigging, and the slosh of the waves against the sides of the boat, and dozens of other tiny and unidentifiable noises that I long since have learned are part of the white sound of sailing. But compared with the disturbance that the engine had been making, it was *silent*. The smell of gasoline and oil went away, too, and that was fine. But it was the silence that felt so good. It was a welcome, lovely silence, and I remember thinking when it first happened, *This must be part of what sailing is all about*.

We sailed along for a while and Mary explained, in very general terms and in an obvious effort not to overload me with too much technical information, how sailing worked. She said that much of the time, the boat didn't get its forward motion from being *pushed* by the wind—although that did happen when you were sailing in the direction the wind was blowing—but rather from the sails' serving as airfoils, just as airplane wings do. The difference in pressure on opposite sides of the sails creates lift, just as for airplanes, and in a sailboat that lift is translated into movement through the water. "But hardly ever in the exact direction you'd like to go," said Mary. "Sailing is almost always a compromise." We had been sailing roughly toward the south bank of the Neuse, and the wind had been coming from the west, down the river, so our sails had been over on the left side of the boat. Mary gradually steered the boat around farther to the left and gave the sails a little more play; large bellies developed in the cloth as it filled with air. Ballooned out like that, the sails looked totally different from those we had been flying a moment before. "We're going pretty much downwind now," said Mary. "We're being pushed along by the wind."

She steered us back to the right, toward the source of the wind, and the sails started flapping. They were not filling with wind as before. Mary pulled in on the lines that controlled the jib and the boom, with its mainsail, and the flapping stopped. She tightened the lines even more and the boat heeled over enough to make me readjust my seating. We also picked up considerable speed. "Airfoil," said Mary. She readjusted the lines, the degree of heel lessened, and I became aware—truly aware, not just intellectually aware—that we probably would not capsize that day. Then Mary said: "Hard alee. Watch your head." As I ducked more than I really needed to, she turned the Typhoon completely toward the wind and pulled in on the lines. For a moment the sails lost all their air and lift; then, as Mary's hand on the tiller took the boat on through its turn, the boom moved across the cockpit and the sails caught the wind on their other sides and snapped smartly taut.

"That was a *tack*," said Mary. "It's also called *coming about*. One of the problems with sailing is that everything has at least two names. We just *came about*. We had been on a *starboard tack*, because the wind was coming from our starboard, our right. Now we're on a *port tack*. Why don't you take it."

There was no question mark at the end of her last sentence, and even before she had finished asking it Mary had slid forward along the cockpit seat and was handing the tiller to me. I took it, and we sailed for a while. To my amazement, I didn't make any major mistakes. With Mary's urging, I experimented with little adjustments to our course, using both the tiller and the sails. I noticed, also to my amazement, that we were zipping right along and that we had come considerably closer to our embarcation point, the entrance to Whittaker Creek, than when Mary had come about. You could go sailing and actually get from one place to another!

I also noticed that the Typhoon was a very responsive boat; that despite its size (although it was small as sailboats go, it remained about as big and heavy as some elephants I have known) it reacted quickly and smoothly when the tiller hand gave it a nudge. I noticed that the relationship among the wind and the sails and the boat and the people on the boat was all very sharp and clear and—dare I say it on my first voyage, when I didn't even know the proper names for the lines and cables that held everything together?— uncomplicated. And I noticed that I was strangely lacking in fear, and I felt strangely in control of the situation. (An unexpected and good-sized puff of wind could have set both those feelings back several notches, but fortunately it didn't come along just then.) I also felt very kindly toward Mary Denmark for undertaking to teach me the way she did.

Later on, I would analyze that day and practically blush at my ignorance of what was going on. I thought I was *sailing*, and on a very crude level I was. But I had no real feeling for the direction from which the wind was coming, the way the sails worked, the proper way to control the sails, how to navigate, how to get back to dry land (Mary took over as we approached the channel), how to get *any-where* I might have wanted to go, or even the proper way to get the sails down. I was, in sum, very fortunate that the Neuse was so wide and that the weather was so good and that my instructor was so perceptive.

But all that was beside the point. The point was that I had fallen in love with sailing. There had been very little provocation that could explain this unusual event, beyond the skill and wisdom of my teacher, who knew that it would do no good, and quite likely do some harm, if she threw everything at me at once. And there was the equally pleasant surprise of discovering that sailing was something that could be done as unpretentiously as hiking in the woods or gliding through the snow; that not only did you not have to belong to a country club in order to sail, you didn't even have to wear a silly cap and pronounce "Yachting" in that dumb way.

CHAPTER THREE

Walloon

It was especially difficult, waiting for Walloon that summer. The almost annual visits to the lake in Michigan had always been the most delightful moments of the year for me and my wife. But I knew that this time there would be sailing. On Walloon Lake there was a sailboat, a boat that had been there all along but that I had always ignored, just as I had ignored all the other aspects of sailing. And the boat was mine to use whenever I wanted it.

Walloon Lake is a long, narrow, unusually clear body of water in what I like to call "Upper Lower Michigan," by which I mean it is in the lower part of Michigan (not on the Upper Peninsula), but it's in the *upper* part of that lower part. If you have trouble with this concept, a quick look at a map will straighten it all out. The map will also show you that there is a good deal of space between the area Walloon's in and the region that often comes to mind when Michigan is mentioned—a region full of places like Ann Arbor, and Detroit, and Grand Rapids, which are clogged with people, factories, pollution, and fast-food franchises. These places are Lower Lower Michigan, and I'm not complaining about them here. It's just that there are still bears and wolverines and unusually clear water in the more northern parts of the state, and not long ago I saw what looked very much like a mountain lion there. There are, in fact, places of wildness and near-wildness in virtually every state of the nation, and their presence tempers my extreme pessimism about what's happening to our environment.

The lake is about ten miles long and it probably averages half a mile in width, with a narrows roughly in its middle and a couple of arms that expand its area considerably. The water is cool and clear-looking, no doubt because much of it comes from springs and because of Michigan's better-than-average record, among the industrial states, of paying attention to the environment. The lake is surrounded by homes, most of them occupied only in the summer and most of them built at a time when people left a little room between themselves and their neighbors. The condo craze has not yet inflicted itself on Walloon, although no doubt there are many promoters and speculators waiting in the wings. A few miles north of the lake is the pleasant small city of Petoskey, which is the seat of the county and center of its trading area and the focus of summer visiting. Petoskey is on Little Traverse Bay, an arm of Lake Michigan, which isn't all that little. A few miles west of Walloon is the smaller town of Charlevoix, which appears to be almost totally supported by the summer trade. Charlevoix is on Lake Michigan, and it has a well-protected harbor that connects with yet another lake, Lake Charlevoix, and so the town is a logical and successful center for boating activities. On a summer day you can

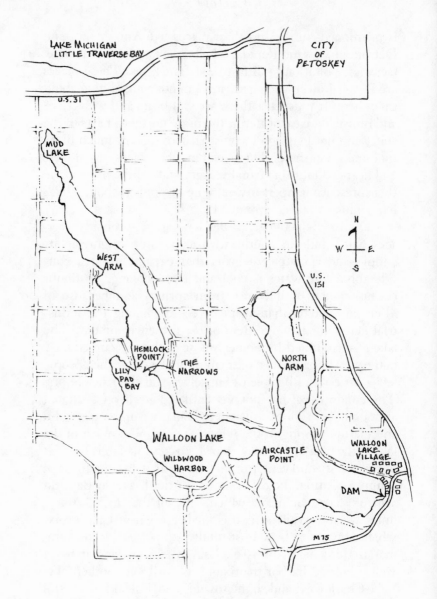

Walloon

stroll along Charlevoix's main street, cut across the municipal park down to the harbor, and see that about half the marine visitors are power boats (I mean *big* power boats: the pearl-white fiber glass monsters that have color television sets and radar and that are larger than some small-town banks) and the other half are sailing vessels.

In both Charlevoix and Petoskey, and in many other towns in Upper Lower Michigan, one of the devices by which the visitors are induced to part with their money is the fudge parlor, where the candy is poured out on marble slabs before one's eyes by clean-cut young people who no doubt double in the wintertime as high school track stars and cheerleaders. Because of the weight which these parlors carry in the summer economy, and because of the attraction they hold for the tourists, the locals for years have referred to the visitors, behind their backs, as "Fudgies." The expression may be on its way out, however; one of the stores in Petoskey has started selling "Fudgie" tee shirts, and such openness about a term of snickering derision is bound to destroy its effectiveness. Furthermore, a long-time resident I know ran a stop sign not long ago and another long-time resident, who didn't know her, shouted "Fudgie!" in contempt. There's nothing that will dilute an epithet faster than applying it to someone who cannot possibly deserve it.

Anyway, the term is rarely used in real anger, and the towners and the summer people in Upper Lower Michigan appear to get along with far less friction than they do in places like the Hamptons on New York's Long Island, Florida's Keys, or portions of Cape Cod. The visitors do manage, however, to avoid knowing very much about the local people who are at the bottom of the socioeconomic scale. While many of the local residents are somewhat successful German-American farming families, there are a lot of very poor people in Upper Lower Michigan, and there are quite a few very poor Indians. The latter escaped almost

all white attention until a few years ago, when the Charlevoix Indians started asserting their fishing rights in Lake
Michigan and even managed to get the white man's judges
to agree with them.

I would have known nothing of Walloon had it not been
for my excellent taste in mothers-in-law. My wife's father,
Jack Morrison, a Chicago newspaperman, after the death
of his first wife married Naomi Kreeger, a Chicagoan who
had a little farm near Lake Walloon. (It ceased to serve as a
full-time working farm some years after my father-in-law
proved that a city boy could get a near-record wheat yield
simply by lavishing more attention and money on it per
acre than had previously been thought possible.) They invited us to the farm in the summers, and we hardly ever
refused. Since Jack's death Naomi has continued issuing
invitations to us and to large numbers of her other friends
and relatives and assorted hangers-on, who would come to
visit for days, weekends, and sometimes extended periods.
You can see the tensions, evident on visitors' faces at the
airport or bus terminal or when we pull into the driveway,
drain away in the lushness of the place. Naomi's cornucopia
of hospitality is an abundant one, including croquet and
badminton, board games, word games (at which she is the
undisputed champion), peace and quiet, sun, flowers, a
vegetable garden, walks in the woods, fishing (with absolutely no chance of disturbing the food chain), great meals,
abundant conviviality, and meditation. And the fleet of
boats.

My father-in-law's deprived city upbringing not only
turned him into a devout and competitive agrarian, it also
gave him a strong appetite for water propulsion, and he
tended to collect boats, which he assembled at a small dock.
He had a sleek craft with an engine more powerful than any
two cars I have owned, and there was a large, raft-type boat

with flat deck and awning, popular on Walloon and neighboring lakes, called a Floteboat, along with several lesser vessels of the tender and bicycle–paddlewheel class. And there was the Ensign, moored a few dozen yards out from the beach in the deeper water so her three feet of keel wouldn't scratch the bottom.

The Ensign is the smallest boat made by the Pearson sailboat people of Rhode Island, now part of the Grumman conglomerate. Naomi's sailboat is twenty-two and a half feet long, and its hull weighs a ton and a half, of which almost one-third is lead, resting down in the keel. The cockpit is quite long, considering the boat's size; this leaves a lot of room outside for passengers, and it means that the cabin, which Pearson literature refers to as a "twin-berth cuddy," is extremely tiny. But for day-sailing on an inland lake, which almost always is sunny-day sailing (or at least starts out that way), there is hardly any need for a cabin at all.

The Ensign's hull is made of fiber glass, and there is a generous supply of teak for the bench seats, railings, and flooring. There are two *headsails*, sails that can be used at the front of the boat: a small one called the *working jib*, for doing the day-to-day work of propelling the boat through the water, regardless of the stiffness of the breeze or the angle of the boat to it, and a large one called the *Genoa*, after a sail that made its appearance in a regatta in the Italian city in 1927. The Genoa is used for achieving better speed in lighter air, among other things. High up on the *mainsail*, the one attached to a track on the mast and, along its lower side, to the boom, is the ensign of the Ensign, a large "E" with six stars arranged in a circle around it.

I had seen the boat at its mooring for years, and I had seen the "E" and the stars a number of times when my father-in-law was alive, for he liked to take the boat out every now and then. I remember being quite leery about going with him, or taking the boat out myself, not because of any lack of skill on his part—he was, in fact, a very good sailor—but because I knew he cherished the boat and I was terrified that I would scratch, sink, or otherwise insult it. There is a certain tension that classically has existed between father- and son-in-law and that involves the father-in-law's favorite possessions (a tension that springs, no doubt, from the fact that the son-in-law has already carried off his daughter), and it is perhaps prudent for a son-in-law to abstain from borrowing his father-in-law's car, golf clubs, power tools, or sailboat. Such prudence was made easier for me, in the case of the sailboat, by the fact that I had always been harboring that burden of ignorant prejudice about sailing and sailors, and that the boat that interested my father-in-law so much interested me not at all.

But that was before I met Mary and Andy in Oriental. When I returned home from that trip, I was full of plans and fantasies about the Ensign. When Naomi issued her invitation for a summer visit to Walloon we replied with unaccustomed promptness, and I found myself calling every week or so to chat and to inquire, in what probably did not come across as a very casual, by-the-way manner, into the Ensign's health. It had made it through the winter okay, I hoped? There were, I assumed, no immediate plans to sell it? Were there other people around or on the way that summer who might be sailing fanatics? (I was selfishly worried about possible competition for the boat's affections. I knew there was a retired gentleman who lived down the lake, a man named Peaslee, who loved to sail the boat and who had done a lot of voluntary upkeep on it through the years. This fellow lived on a strict budget, and he then had no boat of his own, and Naomi had been delighted for him to come up on his motorcycle and take the Ensign "out for a walk," as she put it. Yes, she told me in one of our telephone conversations, Strat Peaslee was sailing the Ensign a lot that summer.)

At the same time I fantasized, I also did a lot of reading up. There is no end of books that purport to explain how to sail, and I purchased far too many of them. I learned a few things, the chief of which was that as writers, a lot of their authors were very good sailors. I yearned for the nautical counterpart to Colin Fletcher's magnificent book on backpacking,* but I didn't find it that summer, nor have I found it since. I discovered also that a lot of what I gleaned from my reading simply didn't sink in, almost certainly because it was not complemented by actual experience. A lot of techniques and maneuvers that are very clear on paper tend to fade from memory when they aren't reinforced by practice.

But the reading continued anyway, because that is what you do when you cannot do what you really want to do. It is the same as with backpacking and ski-touring: When you cannot go out into the woods, you read the words of others who have been there. You go through your worn catalogues in that futile search for equipment that you hope will somehow serve as a substitute for technique and skill, even though you know it cannot. And you study the maps. I have spent many deep winter evenings reading the topographical maps of the Catskills of New York, the Pine Barrens of New Jersey, the Appalachians of North Carolina, planning some trip that might or might not materialize; familiarizing myself with the machine-drawn images of the

---

* Colin Fletcher, *The Complete Walker* (New York: Knopf, 1968), and a reincarnation titled *The New Complete Walker* (New York: Knopf, 1974).

land's features so that when, and if, I got there, I would already have some smattering of a feeling for the place. So it was with sailing. I bought nautical charts, which are bigger and bulkier than topos, and which of course pay far less attention to the features of the land, and I mined them for their information, learned their legends and symbols, taught myself to use their compass roses. And, when I ran across one I particularly liked, I thumbtacked it to the corkboard wall of my office in Brooklyn, sometimes removing one of my beloved topos to make room.

It was overkill, pure and simple. Walloon Lake was so small that no nautical chart paid it serious mind. It was just a minor embellishment on *National Ocean Survey Chart Number 14913: United States, Great Lakes, Lake Michigan, Grand Traverse Bay to Little Traverse Bay*. The chart showed quite clearly that, although one end of Walloon came to within a few hundred yards of Lake Michigan, and another was less than four miles from Lake Charlevoix, the little lake was effectively sealed off from the rest of the watery world. You could sail a lifetime on Walloon and never find a passage to the lakes and oceans beyond.

But that was not the point. I studied the charts, and I read the books, not just in anticipation of the brief vacation with the Ensign, but as part of something else that I was quite incapable of explaining, but that I knew, in some vague but certain way, had something to do with an urge to learn how to sail, an urge to become a sailor.

Naomi, who is very good at recognizing and appreciating people's whims and fancies and driving ambitions, had Made Arrangements. She is very good at Making Arrangements. She had told Strat Peaslee, the retired gentleman from down the lake, that I was coming and that I was particularly interested in sailing the Ensign. Not long after we arrived at the farm so did Strat, with a suggestion that we go boating.

Strat Peaslee is a quiet, friendly man of the sort that you do not often encounter in New York City—by which I mean that if he is self-centered, he keeps it to himself. He is the opposite of brusque, and whenever he does something he seems to consider first what effects it might have on others. Although he has never said it to me in so many words, Strat seems to be one of those folks who, having been taught as a child that you do unto other people as you would have them do unto you, decided to live by that rule, and who would find it extremely uncomfortable to live otherwise.

He is what is called "slight" in stature—a rather short and unfleshy man who probably weighs no more than a hundred and twenty-five pounds—and he is in his early sixties and has eyes of the sort that seem to twinkle. He has a fine sense of humor, almost of the droll Yankee variety, and you have to be careful when he is speaking lest you miss a fine pun or the buildup to a punchline that will be delivered without fanfare, almost *sotto voce*, but that will lose nothing in the process. We got along fine from the very beginning.

Strat lives a couple of miles down the lake as the heron flies, but several more miles by the roads that twist around Walloon. He lives with and takes care of his mother, who is in her nineties, in one of the older houses that borders the lake. For years Strat lived in Defiance, Ohio, where he worked in a paint store. Not long before I met him, Strat and his wife had become divorced and he left his job and moved to Upper Lower Michigan. It is not exactly retirement for him, since he is anything but wealthy and not the sort of person who enjoys not working, anyway. But to an outsider Strat's life looks pretty good, what with his living directly on a very nice lake and his sailing the Ensign with some frequency.

Strat gets around on a Kawasaki motorcycle. When he rides the machine he wears heavy cycling boots, a jacket, and one of those crash helmets that has a blackened plastic visor, and if you saw this slight figure zooming down the road, you would assume he was a teen-ager—at least until he stopped and removed his helmet and revealed his grey hair. Even then, if you caught his lively eyes you might wonder if he were a teen-ager in grey-haired-man's clothing.

We sailed a lot in the next two weeks. And Strat taught me a lot. Whatever fears I may have had about competition between us for the sailboat were unfounded, and I was keenly disappointed when a day came around when Strat couldn't make it. (I was supposed to be working when I was at the farm, and I really should have welcomed those days. Free-lance writers generally cannot afford to take regular vacations, but they often find themselves *working* in places that are, shall we say, very refreshing. I had a typewriter set up in an outbuilding on a hill a hundred yards or so from the farmhouse. Unfortunately, the typewriter was in front of a window that looked out over the lake. The Ensign's mooring was clearly visible from my typing chair.)

Like Mary Denmark, Strat was an excellent teacher. He achieved this, as she had, largely through not acting very much like a teacher. He was self-effacing and low key, and it was obvious that he did not believe there was just one correct way to do something. A typical Peaslee explanation of a sailing maneuver would start out, "Now, I'm not sure this is the best way to do such-and-such, but it's what they taught me, and it seems to work." Gradually the wall that I had painstakingly constructed out of prejudice, ignorance, and stereotype—the association of sailing with Prussian snobbery—crumbled.

Strat also skillfully blended his verbal explanations with physical demonstrations, and in sailing that is not at all easy. Like many sports that are combinations of physical and intellectual endeavor, sailing does not allow itself to be neatly divided into "classroom" and "field" segments. The best way to learn about the techniques of sailing probably consists of a reasonable, but not overwhelming, amount of reading up and dry-land discussion, followed by a great amount of practical experimentation. You can read all day about how to go from a starboard tack to a port tack, and you can illustrate it on graph paper with little arrows that indicate the oncoming wind, and you can discuss the matter earnestly with a competent instructor. But the lesson can never be complete until you have come about, and done it repeatedly, in a sailboat out on the water and in the wind. Strat knew all this, and so I did a lot of my learning in the water, through trial and error, with the emphasis on error.

The teaching of sailing is further impeded by the fact that often when things happen on a sailboat—when direction is changed, or when you return to the dock or your mooring—they happen quickly. Frequently the events occur faster than they can be discussed rationally by teacher and student. The inevitable maneuver of approaching a mooring, for example, is often a slow and even boring process up until the final thirty seconds, at which time it can change into a situation that ranges from Very Busy to Pandemonium. It is commonplace for new sailors (and old ones, too, for that matter) who are sailing with the wind more or less behind them to let the wind get too far on the wrong side of the boat, with the result being an involuntary *jibe*, in which the boom and mainsail swing wildly across the deck.

It should not be surprising, in such situations, that the instructor would lack the words to explain quickly enough what needs to be done, and to snatch the tiller or line from the student in frantic exasperation and to do it him- or herself. This may prevent an unwanted event from occurring—it may insure a proper and safe landing at the mooring, and it may keep someone's head and the boat's mast from being cracked by the jibe—but it also may result in the student's feeling like a dummy. A good teacher anticipates all these events and plans for them and does his or her best to prepare the student for them, and furthermore makes every effort to protect the student's ego, which can become very fragile when trying to learn how to sail. Such teachers must be quite rare, and I was fortunate that Strat Peaslee was one of them.

In the case of the Ensign, Strat's job was made more difficult (but the sailing education made more effective) by two facts: Walloon Lake is long and narrow, and it is bordered by hills and pastures.

The first fact meant that we had to do a lot of course-changing whenever we sailed. Rarely did the prevailing wind favor trips straight up or down the lake; far more often, to get where we were going we had to follow a zig-zag course of tacks. And the more tacking I did, the more I learned about sailing.

The second fact has also to do with the wind. Because of the variety of terrain around the lake, the wind can never be counted on to come from any one direction. There is generally a prevailing wind—sort of the wind-of-the-day—and as often as not it is a zephyr, a wind that had just crossed Lake Michigan from out of the northwest, so that it pushes from Naomi's end of the lake down toward the other. But there are several, sometimes dozens of, other winds, little local puffs and miscellaneous breezes that come tumbling down off an open space or shooting out of a cove.

And there are patches of water that are free of any wind at all, for they are protected by hills or stands of tall trees.

A sailboat passing by is protected, as well, until it passes out of the wind-shadow of the hill. Then it's possible to get socked hard and unexpectedly by a puff of the prevailing wind or one of the local drafts. Such conditions can be nerve-wracking, but they also are excellent for the student sailor, for they offer continual—and sometimes continuous—variety, and they make it impossible for the person whose hand is on the tiller to become bored or complacent.

Because of these phenomena, I was learning early on an important lesson about becoming a sailor: that sailing conditions vary a great deal, and unless you want to be strictly a fair-weather sailor, restricted to a single boat on a single patch of water, you will have to make yourself ready for anything. When I went out into the Neuse with Mary Denmark, there was plenty of deep water in all directions. The wind was steady and fairly predictable, and when it blew from a certain direction it tended to keep blowing from that same direction. You could set the boat on a course and stay there a while. On Walloon, and no doubt on many other lakes of comparable size, you had constantly to anticipate changes in the velocity and direction of the wind, and you had to anticipate changes in your own direction because of the narrowness of the lake. Both experiences had a lot to do with the definition I was forming of *sailing*. I was fortunate enough to have been exposed to both of them early in my sailing career.

I wondered, on those days when Walloon's wind was calm and when the surprises were minimal, about the other forms of sailing that I had *not* yet experienced. Half a mile away was the second largest of the Great Lakes, a headstrong body of water said to command the deepest respect even of those who make their living sailing on the most unpredictable oceans. And what of the waters of the Atlantic and Pacific themselves? I thought of Oriental, and of all that water and shoreline in the Neuse and in Pamlico Sound that I had not yet seen. What experiences would these places offer?

I dug out a Rand McNally road atlas one night and amused myself with the discovery that—theoretically, at least—it is possible to haul the Ensign out of Walloon, trail her a couple of miles to the shore of Lake Charlevoix, sail up to Lake Michigan, run down to Chicago, and then do a bit of river-sailing, with assistance from an outboard, along the Chicago Sanitary and Ship Canal, Illinois and Michigan Canal, Des Plaines and Illinois Rivers; into the Mississippi at St. Louis; through the Gulf of Mexico; around the Florida Keys (or, if I were in a hurry and could sublimate my feelings about the damage done to Florida by the ditch-diggers, across the state via canals and Lake Okeechobee); then up the East Coast by way of the Intracoastal Waterway; into lower New York Harbor; hang a right at Governor's Island, and finally tie up at the remnants of an abandoned dock at the foot of Sackett Street in Brooklyn, a few blocks from my home.

△ △ △

Almost every day when there was wind, and on more than one occasion when the day ended with none, we sailed the lake. Sometimes Strat and I went out for long spells, sometimes for brief runs after work. The wind-of-the-day had a habit of dying down in the late afternoon, and if we were on the water then we had a good opportunity to discuss some of the finer points of what I was learning, free of panics caused by puffs and jibes. Slowly the basic facts of sailing started to sink in, and slowly I found myself better able to anticipate situations such as tacking and docking without devoting too much conscious thought to them. It is much the same in any learning process, I suppose; what once seemed awkward and maybe even impossible, you realized one day, had become something approaching second nature.

Of course, it was not only by any means all work, or anything even approaching all work. Sailing with Strat was a great learning process, but it was also a great deal of fun. It was good for the eye, the nose, the ears, the brain, the digestion, and the emotional system; it was an especially enriching experience. Strat summed it up one fine, cloudless day with an expression that I have heard several times since. We were running downwind, leaning back in the cockpit with not much to do, and he said: "I wonder what the poor folks are doing today." It was clear when he said it that it had nothing to do with putting down poor people or with being the sort of society-snob yachtsman that I once deplored so strongly. Rather, it was an assertion that when you're sailing, *everybody* is somehow poorer than you.

Somewhere along in there I soloed. It is strange, but I don't remember the occasion in great detail. I may have progressed far enough in my informal lessons with Strat so that taking the boat out by myself was simply the logical next thing to do. I do remember that it was a fine, sunny day with a light-to-moderate breeze from the northwest, and that I was at a good pausing place in my work, and that Strat had called to say he couldn't come by that day. So I went down to the dock, rowed out to the mooring, got aboard the Ensign, and sailed away. It seemed like a perfectly normal, natural thing to do. Tacking went well, and I didn't jibe inadvertently, and I had a fine time in all respects until I started back.

Then I remembered that I would have to approach the mooring all by myself, with no one to help. The mooring was a float, about the size of a large pumpkin, anchored to the lake's bottom by a chain, that had at its top a metal ring about five inches in diameter. At the bow of the boat was a chain that ended in a shackle. The trick was to bring the boat, sails flapping and headed into the wind, slowly and smoothly up to the float and, at precisely the right moment, to lean over the side or off the bow and snap the shackle onto the ring. Once this connection was made the Ensign was fast to the mooring and the sailor could drop the sails and pack things away. The shackle-and-ring maneuver, however, offered very little margin for error. If you missed the float at the end of your approach, you had to turn the boat away (for you were usually headed toward shallow water, and you could run aground in a dozen yards), get wind into your sails again so you would be able to control the boat, and circle around and try again. When two or more people were aboard, it was relatively easy for one of them to steer and handle the sails while the other worked the shackle. But a single-hander had to do both, and part of the routine required that at the last minute, he must let go of the tiller and go forward to snap the shackle. For a short period of time, then, the boat would not be under control.

The whole thing sounds difficult, and as I returned to the Ensign's end of the lake on my first solo it sounded impossible. But for some reason, I caught the ring on the first try. I realized then, more than at any other time, that Strat had taught me, and that I had learned, a lot about sailing.

But by the time I left Petoskey that summer I knew, too, that there was an enormous amount that I had not learned. Even though Strat told me it was possible to gauge the wind's direction just from the sensation on one's neck or cheeks or forehead, I knew that I had no such sense. And this really bothered me, for if one were not conversant with the direction of the wind, how could one sail? Nor could I really tell when a jibe was about to happen. It seemed that nothing came naturally, or smoothly, or instinctively. And surely in sailing there is much that should come in those ways, or else the sport is nothing but work.

But I felt I had *started* to learn and feel these things. Sometimes, when you are learning something new and totally foreign, you realize that, even though the knowledge has not yet arrived, it is not far away and it *will* arrive someday—that the learning process is at work and functioning properly and that the brain and hands may be clumsy now but that they are learning, getting better. After sailing at Petoskey for a couple of weeks, I still could not say that I was certain that the knowledge was on the way. But I could feel bits and pieces of it soaking into my brain and into my body's rusting motor, and it was comforting to realize that maybe an old dog *was* beginning to learn some new tricks. At the very least I had learned a lot of the terminology, the nomenclature of sailing. The nuts and bolts were becoming more understandable to me; the tangles of masts and riggings no longer looked like tangles, but rather they seemed now to have purposes, functions, and order.

2

NUTS AND BOLTS

△△△

CHAPTER FOUR

The Language of the Boat

One of the first things that happens when you're learning to sail is that you realize you must learn a new language—or at least a new vocabulary for the language you already possess.

Each vocation and avocation has its own means of communication, and as human life becomes more cluttered and complicated with technological change, or at least predictions of technological change, the languages become more difficult for outsiders to decipher. Physicians and lawyers have always spoken in strange tongues, the better to baffle and awe their customers, but now practically everyone is in on the act, from computer programmers to fast-food merchandisers. Much of the language serves only to keep potentially inquisitive outsiders at bay, and upon examination it is quickly revealed to be silly and needless. Is it really necessary for a policeman to engage in a sing-song recital of what "the alleged perpetrator" may or may not have done, or for a legal document to refer repeatedly to "the party of the first part"? And is it not a little foolish-sounding for a weekend sailor to speak of the tightly-packed kitchen section of a cruising sailboat as the "galley" or to the even more tightly-packed toilet as the "head"? Isn't it likely that someone who spends the great majority of her or his time on dry land will even lose precious moments trying to remember that it's *starboard* that's on the right? Isn't there the chance that someone who does use the nautical terms will be viewed as one given to affectations, the sort of person who sports little caps and speaks of "Yachting"?

Yes, such possibilities do exist. But in sailing, as in all the other callings whose practitioners have dreamed up special words and phrases and imposed them on themselves and their fellows, there is at least the glimmer of a valid reason why the confusing terms are there.

One of the definitions of sailing that is in wide use goes something like this: Long periods of utter boredom, interspersed with moments of extreme terror. You can sail for half an hour, half a day, half a week, and very little happens. But very frequently when something does happen, as it invariably will, it happens in a hurry. Sailors must be able to communicate quickly, not only with the others in the boat or elsewhere (in the boat you're about to slam into, for instance, or on the dock you're approaching and that a fierce current is trying to carry you away from), but also with your own mind. If everything on and about the boat has a fairly precise name, and everyone involved knows what that name is, then a lot of time can be saved and a lot of mistakes left unmade. Compare the following two requests, which add up to the same thing:

1. "Do you see that rope over there? No, the one next to it. Yes. Would you please wrap it around that shiny drum that sticks up on that side of the boat and then pull on

it until the sail it's attached to gets pulled in some more? No, the other way. Clockwise around the drum. Right. One or two turns are fine. And pull it in until the sail stops flapping like that? And then put the rope where it comes off the drum—make sure it's still tight—put it into the metal slot with the teeth on the side and with the palm of your hand push down on the rope until it gets jammed in the slot? That's right. Yes, it'll hold it just fine if you tuck it down firmly enough. Thanks."

2. "The jib seems to be luffing a little. Would you please sheet it in? Thanks."

The precision of the sailing language helps almost as much within your own mind, particularly if you are less than a full-time sailor and therefore unlikely to devote a majority, or even very much, of your time to thinking about sailing. *We're luffing; need to sheet in the jib* has a certain economy when you run it through your mind, just as it does when you're making the request out loud to your sailing partner.

While much of the language of sailing has to do with specific physical items on the boat and in the marine environment, a lot of it also has to do with the routines, techniques, and maneuvers that go into sailing from one place to another. What follow are lists of some of these items and actions. This is by no means a comprehensive exploration of the language; rather, it is more like one of those thirty-minute cassettes that purport to teach you enough of a foreign language to get you a taxicab, a meal, a john, a hotel, and the American Express office when you're traveling. The "Sources" listing at the end of the book will steer you toward publications that can provide much more elaborate translations. And remember: In sailing, perhaps more than in any other occupation or diversion that uses a specialized language, there are multiple names for just about everything. It is around the time when you have clearly understood the difference between a "mast" and a "boom" that someone will start speaking to you of "spars." The only thing to do is persevere, and wait for the day when you can throw nautical language around with similar abandon.

In this listing, the nuts and bolts are grouped into three main categories. One concerns the parts of the boat itself; one deals with the terminology of sailing the boat; the third deals with the nomenclature of navigation, my own personal definition of which is getting from one place to another without being overly surprised that you got there.

Even before getting to the specific nooks, crannies, bilges and battens of the boat itself, one has to wade through a volume or two of definitions of *boats*. And for many of them, the meanings are a little vague and they overlap at just about the time you think you've got them figured out.

For one thing, boats are not *ships*. There is no precise definition of a ship, but everyone seems to agree that they are much larger than boats; certainly large enough for travel on the ocean. If you are interested in sailing a ship, or in buying one, maybe you should reconsider reading this book.

Yachts, despite all the connotations and stereotypes, are any privately-owned boats that are used for pleasure. Moving quickly past the sub-category of motor yachts, which sailing people often refer to as "stinkpots," we come to *sailing vessels*, which are any vessels that sail. And that brings us face-to-face with a huge cornucopia (or Pandora's box, if you're a stinkpotter who doesn't think too highly of the "ragwavers" that clutter up the harbor).

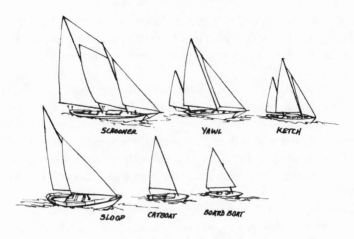

Some sailing rigs

Sailing vessels are included in the general category called *small craft*. They can be *multihulls*, which usually refers to twin-hulled *catamarans* and three-hulled *trimarans*; they can be *motor sailers*, or vessels that look like, and are, compromises between motor yachts, with their creature comforts and engine-powered mobility, and sailboats, with their ability to take advantage of the wind. Motor sailers are the Winnebagos of sailing, and I don't necessarily mean that in a disparaging way.

Many sailboats of all sorts are also, technically and legally, motorboats if they contain, or have attached to their backsides, motors. But in sailing language such boats are usually referred to as *auxiliaries*, in recognition of the fact that the engines are there only in a supporting role.

Cruiser, when applied to either sailing or motor boats, means the boat has accommodations for overnight use; when someone speaks of a *cruising sailboat* she almost always means a sailboat with an enclosed cabin and space for sleeping and for at least the minimal nutritional and hygienic pursuits. This probably means a boat of more than 22 or 24 feet in length, although there's nothing to stop a boat builder from referring to something much smaller as a "pocket cruiser."

It would be very difficult to spend the night on a *board boat*, which resembles a surfboard in length, width, and accommodations. In fact, it is unusual to even go sailing on a board boat without getting wet, since you sit but a couple of inches above, and often several inches below, the surface of the water. The Sunfish and Sailfish are members of this category. Increasingly, though, people refer to "board boats" when they are talking about *boardsailing* on *sailboards*, which are the true genetic offspring of surfboards and which require that the sailor stand up on them (and even hold up the mast) in what is called *windsurfing*.

Board boats are usually part of the *catboat* family. A catboat has one mast and one sail, and the sail is not always triangular in shape. *Sailing dinghies* are dinghies (small boats used for rowing about, fishing, or getting to and from larger boats that are at anchor) with sailing rigs on them, and the rigs often fall into the catboat category.

Among the larger sailboats, we sometimes encounter a *ketch*. This means a sailing boat with two masts. The smaller and shorter one, called the *mizzenmast*, is behind the *mainmast*, but it rises out of the boat in front of the tiller. For some reason, the same sort of boat with a mizzenmast to the rear of the tiller is called a *yawl*. And if the masts are equal in size or if the rear one is the taller, what you have is a *schooner*. And, almost certainly, a lot of money.

This leaves us with one remaining general classification of sailboat, and that is the one that has figured most in my education and that is more than likely to be what comes to your mind when you think of ordinary, pleasure sailing: the *sloop*. A sloop is a sailing vessel with one mast and two sails. Both sails depend on the mast for support, and one flies in front of and one behind the mast. The sails are usually triangular, although they don't have to be.

So, we have a basic sloop in front of us, rocking easily in the water. To learn some of the nomenclature of the boat itself, it is convenient to break the category down again, this time into two arbitrary sub-categories: the hull, and the sails, spars, and rigging.

△ △ △

The *hull* is the basic body of the boat. It can be made of wood, fiber glass, metal, canvas stretched over wooden ribs as in the traditional canoe, or even cement. Strictly speaking, the hull is only the structural framework of the boat, the thing that holds everything else together, but we're stretching the definition a little here to include some of the things that are added to the basic body.

When the boat is loaded normally, the line that is formed from front to rear by the water is its *waterline*. Descriptions of sailboats will frequently refer to their *l.w.l.*, which is the commonly-used abbreviation for a boat's *length on the waterline*. The boat's *l.o.a.* is its *overall length*, or *length over all*. The *beam* is the width of the boat at its widest part; if a boat appears wider than you think it should be, you may refer to the entire boat as "beamy." *Freeboard* is the distance from the waterline to the top of the boat, while *draft* is the distance from the waterline to the bottommost point of the vessel. (You say a boat has "Three feet of draft," or that "She draws three feet.")

The boat's *bow* is its front end, and if there's a system of rails up there that'll keep you from falling off it's called a *bow pulpit*, although purists may insist that the name applies only to a combination of planks and rails that actually extends out in front of the boat's bow, over the water. At the

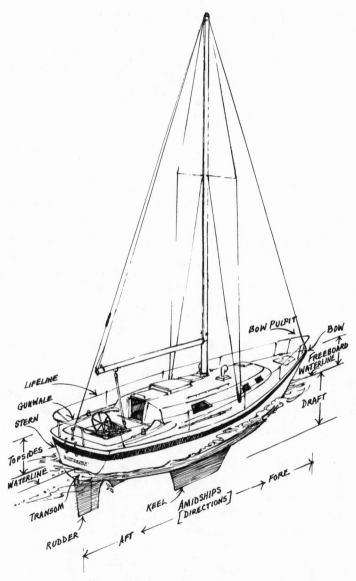

BOW PULPIT

BOW

FREEBOARD

WATERLINE

LIFELINE

DRAFT

GUNWALE

STERN

TOPSIDES

WATERLINE

FORE

TRANSOM

KEEL

AMIDSHIPS
[DIRECTIONS]

RUDDER

AFT

Some parts of the hull

other end is the *stern*, and the structural member that forms it (and that is vertical or pretty much so) and that holds everything together at that end is the *transom*. When you set off for the front of the boat you are headed *fore*; when you head *aft* you are going toward the *after* section. In the middle of all this, right where you'd expect to find it, is the region known as *amidships*.

The sides of the hull above the waterline are the *topsides*, and at the top of them, at the line where the hull meets the deck, are the *gunwales* (pronounced GUNnels). Often the gunwales are topped by narrow *toe rails* that define the junction between deck and topsides and that provide some footing security for sailors. Further protection may be offered by *lifelines*, which are cables that extend around and a couple of feet above the deck's perimeter.

At the very bottom of the hull, at least in many small boats and in virtually all large ones, is the most fascinating part of the sailboat's structure: the *keel*.

Keels come in two basic configurations: fixed and non-fixed. Non-fixed keels are ones that are easily moveable upward and downward by the sailor, like aircraft landing gear, and they are usually found on smaller sailboats (although some cruising boats have them; for every rule in sailing, there are at least a dozen exceptions). The non-fixed variety includes *centerboards*, which pivot about a pin and are raised and lowered into the water beneath the boat (usually through a slot in the center of the boat) by a cable or line, and *daggerboards*, which look something like their name and are shoved manually down through the slot and usually held in place by friction and gravity. The sailing board boats, such as Sunfish and Phantoms, use daggerboards. The boards employed in moveable keel boats are often no more than tapered pieces of wood, with no weight added.

Fixed keels, too, sort themselves into two main groups.

Sailboats with *deep keels* have weighted projections extending pretty much the length of their hulls, tapering into the water at the bow and sweeping back to their largest, and heaviest, dimension back near the stern. *Fin keels*, which are more likely to be seen on sloops (but which won't be unless the boats are out of the water or the viewer is swimming under it), are projections from the center of the hull's bottom that resemble fish fins. They also resemble daggerboards that have been put into place. Boats with deep keels (or "long keels," as some call them) are generally better at tracking through the water, while fin keels produce more nimble, touchy maneuvering.

There is a major difference between fixed keels and the other sort, and that is that fixed keels have *ballast*—extra, added weight, usually lead—added to and made part of them.

The amount of ballast is correlated directly with the size of the boat. Mary Denmark's Cape Dory Typhoon, less than 19 feet (l.o.a.), has a full keel that carries 900 pounds of lead. Other boats in that general category may have 500 or even fewer pounds. Cape Dory's 30-foot ketch, a cruising vessel that can go virtually anywhere, has 4,000 pounds of lead tucked into its keel.

The reason ballast is there, and the reason keels are there, is stability, one definition of which might be the freedom from turning over, scuttling sideways, or scaring yourself and your passengers silly. The stability of a sailboat depends on a lot of factors, not the least of which is good seamanship, but one of the major components is the keel. This bottommost part of the boat does its job on two fronts.

One of them, which really has more to do with the sort of navigational stability that gets you where you want to go, involves sideways motion. Among the first things that you learn about sailing, and that I started to learn in Oriental and discovered more about on Lake Walloon, is that the wind hardly ever just pushes you along from the rear. And when the wind is coming from directly in front of you, you aren't going anywhere. (Remember? When you want to bring everything to a halt, as you do when you're raising or lowering the sails, you head directly into the wind.) The wind is always coming from the side—maybe from a shallow angle (from 10 o'clock or 2 o'clock, if you visualize the boat on the face of an old-fashioned, non-digital clock with 12 at the bow), or from a big angle (from 3 or 9 o'clock, say). And, while you're adjusting your sails so as to make the best use of that wind, which in the majority of cases means generating airfoil-type lift, you are using that wind from the side in order to achieve forward motion. The keel helps make all this possible.

The wind, striking the boat and its sails from the side, wants to push the whole thing to the opposite side. And so it would, if it were not for the efforts the sailor is making to steer in another direction and for the counteracting pressure of the keel. Sitting down there in the water like a broad spatula blade, the keel takes that sideways energy and converts it—or some of it—into forward energy. (It isn't able to convert it all, and the result is that the boat *makes leeway*, which is a proposition that will be discussed later.)

These forces and counterforces are manifested most when the wind's angle with the boat most approaches the perpendicular—when it comes from around 3 or 9 o'clock. When the push comes from nearly directly behind the boat (from maybe 5:30 or 6:30 o'clock), the keel doesn't provide much of this sort of help at all. In fact, on board boats with non-fixed keels the routine is to pull up the board when traveling in this fashion, which is called *running*, and which also will be discussed later.

The other front on which the keel performs so heroically has a direct relationship to the sort of stability that comes first and most frequently to the beginning sailor's mind: the stability that prevents capsize. Picture it: a relatively small hull out on a relatively large pond (or lake, or ocean), with a mast sticking up that's taller than the boat is long. Attached to the mast are two sails, whose sole *raison d'être* is to catch wind. We know that the wind pushes against the sails and that down below, the keel helps translate that sideways push into forward motion. But what about the tendency of that wind–sail combination to just push the boat, keel and all, farther and farther to the side until the afternoon is totally ruined? And, to make matters worse, paint into the imaginary picture a number of large, unforgiving waves. They don't have keels, and so the wind is pushing them in only one direction, and so they're slapping relentlessly against the boat too. And their slapping motion, coming as it does from the same side as the wind, seems contrived to throw the boat over as well.

The keel comes to the rescue here. The reason for this is rather complicated, and it is the sort of thing that engineers enjoy plotting on mathematical calculators. But on a very elementary level here is what happens:

The boat possesses two very important centers, a center of gravity and a center of buoyancy. The center of gravity is the center of the boat's mass—the point at which, if you could put your finger on it, the boat would balance perfectly. The center of buoyancy is a little harder to visualize. It is the center of gravity of the water that the boat is displacing by being in the lake, pond, or ocean. As a lawyer-sailor named John McPhee explained it in an article in *Sail* magazine in March, 1982, "The center of buoyancy is the sum of all the upward and inward pressures exerted by the ocean trying to rush in and fill each cubic inch of the depression in the water made by your hull."

The two invisible but very real points work as levers on each other whenever the boat heels over, as it does in wind or wave action or even when the crew shifts its position. In a boat with a weighted, fixed keel, the center of gravity is rather low—below the waterline—and its position is constant. The location of the center of buoyancy changes, depending on the boat's degree of heel. The relationship of the two centers is such that, while a certain degree of heel is permitted, a *great* degree of it is resisted, and an even greater degree of heel is resisted with even greater force. The more the boat heels, the more the keel, with its weight and its center of gravity, fights further heel. The result (at least according to the people with calculators) is that a real capsize is very unlikely. In fact, when one does occur—usually as the product of very strong waves—the forces inherent in such boats are such that the vessels will turn all the way over and then come back upright. The process, which I have not yet enjoyed but which must be a real conversation piece, is called *turning turtle*.

None of the foregoing applies equally to the centerboard and daggerboard boats, or to any boat with an unweighted keel. On them, the relationship between centers of gravity and buoyancy is radically different from that on a boat with a heavy keel. The center of gravity is quite high, and capsizes are something you plan for. At the same time, most of the smaller boats are designed so that when capsizes occur, the boats may be righted easily and quickly.

What, you may now ask, is so fascinating about all that? What keels do may be interesting, may be quite essential. But fascinating? Consider this:

Keels determine where you go when you go sailing, and thus they determine, to a very great extent, just what sort of a sailor you're going to be. Sailing is chock-full of tradeoffs—being pushed sideways in order to go forward, being treated to sheer terror alternating with utter boredom, reduced privacy and comfort in exchange for moments of pure ecstasy. But perhaps the most meaningful of them (certainly the most meaningful to me) is the tradeoff in mobility that is imposed by the thing that sticks down on the underside of your boat.

There is nothing more certain in sailing than the fact that if you take a boat into water that is shallower than the boat is deep, you will run aground. Strictly speaking, it's the boat's overall *draft* we're talking about here, but the keel is a major constituent in a boat's draft. If you want to sail across the Atlantic without exciting front-page interest around the world, you will probably do it in a vessel with a lot of length, weight, and draft. If you want to sport around of an afternoon on one of Cape Cod's small fresh-water ponds, your best bet is a board boat with removable daggerboard; with anything else you'd be restricted to the very middle of the pond where the water is deepest. If you want to go sailing a couple of miles away in Cape Cod Bay, that thirty-some-odd-mile stretch of protected salt water between the Cape and mainland Massachusetts, you'd want a boat with more of a keel, for, while the bay is relatively protected when compared with the Atlantic Ocean, it is not at all immune to waves and winds.

The tradeoffs do not end there. If you want to sail your boat on Cape Cod Bay, where will you dock or moor it? There are a few harbors that can accept boats with considerable draft, but not all that many. A lot of boaters prefer to tie up in the small town harbors, which are protected but where the water is shallower. That brings up a further complication: The tidal range—the difference between the height of the water at low and at high tides—is relatively pronounced along the New England coast, and in some of Cape Cod's small harbors the water level slips down to just a few inches at low tide. Twice a day, tidal inlets that were dozens of yards wide and six feet deep become shallow streamlets. What happens then with a keel boat? It can run aground without going anywhere, even at anchor; the water will become shallower beneath its very keel. In some places, even boats without keels can't traverse the few hundred yards between marina and bay at low tide. Kids who grow up on Sunfish and Penguins in such waters learn that they must be back from an outing not in time for lunch or the Little League game but rather in time to get through the inlet into the harbor before the water's all gone.

Chesapeake Bay and Maryland's Eastern Shore are subject to much less pronounced tidal variations, but a boat's draft still controls the sort of sailing that can be done. A crossing of the bay itself from, say, one of the many harbors on the western side, over toward Washington, across the deep water and then up one of the dozens of lovely and not-yet-spoiled rivers on the eastern peninsula, can take a sailboat through waves and wind that might rival those on the open ocean. In such conditions, a heavy keel and plenty of draft would be helpful. But once arrived on the other side, the sailor might want to explore as deeply as possible into the tidal rivers, with their colonial farmlands and dense woods and occasional riverside towns and villages. How far "as deeply as possible" is will depend directly on the boat's draft. If it is four feet (very handy for crossing the bay) it means the boat can go no farther upstream than the point where the water at low tide will drop to no less than four feet deep. It may mean, too, that the boat's stopping place for the night must be at the end of an anchor, out in the deeper water, rather than close to the shore. It is one of the paradoxes of sailing that the sailboat, which promises a much closer degree of communication with nature than the noisy, smelly world of power boating, often requires— because of its extreme dependence on water that isn't too shallow—that its devotees remain at arm's length from the earth.

The keel and draft control a sailor's mobility in other ways, as well. For one example: Fixed-keel boats are heavier than comparable boats with non-fixed keels, and they are harder to move around on land. A sailor with a moveable-keel boat can, more than likely, transport it on a trailer with greater ease and less strain on his car's engine, and thus can visit more varied bodies of water.

Several efforts have been made to deal with the limitations of keels, but none has provided what you'd call the perfect solution. Cruisers usually carry some kind of subsidiary boat—a dinghy or inflatable of some sort—to facilitate trips in to land for recreation, nature study, raids on grocery stores, and, in the case of Maryland's Eastern Shore, pigging-out sessions at the region's famed crab houses. And some sailboats come with both fixed and non-fixed keels. There is a keel along the bottom of the boat that is shallow enough to admit it to quiet creeks and sandy beaches, and which is weighted sufficiently to provide stability. But in the middle of the keel is the slot for a pivoted centerboard, which in deeper water will come into play to provide help in keeping on, literally, an even keel. Draft in such boats can be changed from as little as one or two feet to as much as five or six.

And the sailboat can be built as many are in England, where the tidal range is quite severe. These boats have two fixed keels, each projecting outward from the hull at an angle. When the tide goes out, the boat won't be able to sail anywhere, but neither will it fall over, since it will be resting comfortably on two broad stilts.

If you follow the keel to its rearmost point, you may run into the *rudder*—or, if it isn't there, it will be a little farther on at the very stern of the boat, attached to the transom. The rudder is a moveable board that is used to steer the boat. It is connected either through the hull or around the transom to a stick, called the *tiller*, that the sailor holds. The whole thing is useless when the boat is standing still, but when it moves, and water starts rushing past the rudder, a pull or push on the tiller will disturb the water pattern and pivot the boat around to one direction or another. When you're going foward, moving the tiller toward one side of the boat will cause the boat to turn toward the opposite direction.

Sometimes, especially on larger boats, the part of the tiller is played by a *wheel*, which is geared to make turning easier and which turns like an automobile's steering wheel. Like a car and unlike a tiller, a wheel turned in one direction makes the boat turn toward that same direction.

The entire steering apparatus is referred to as the *helm*, and the person who does the steering is called the *helmsman*. The expression "helmswoman" is hardly ever heard, so if you want to be non-sexist in these matters it's perfectly all right to refer to the person at the tiller as the *skipper*. The skipper is the person on the boat who is in charge; who gives orders (but who does not push other people around, since the days of mutiny are not yet over). The only person on a sailboat who can reasonably be in a position to give orders is the person at the helm, since he or she is in ultimate control of where the boat is going.

The skipper, along with anyone else who wants to, sits in the *cockpit*, which is a sunken portion of the deck, usually well aft, but sometimes amidships on larger boats. If there's a raised edge around the cockpit to keep water out, it's called a *coaming*. If the cockpit has drain holes that automatically carry off water, it is *self-bailing*; the holes are called *scuppers*.

Forward of the cockpit (in most sloops, at least) may be found the region that goes by the name of *below*. This refers, in the case of boats big enough to have decks, to everything that exists beneath them—the engine compartment, facilities for eating, sleeping, and sanitation, and storage. In small boats, whose decks enclose only a tiny storage space, the enclosure may be called a *cuddy*. On larger boats, it is the *cabin*.

To get to the cabin, you walk through the *hatchway* and down the *companionway*, which is a ladder or steps. Once inside, you enter a small world in which virtually nothing seems to have a dry-land name. The ceiling is an *overhead*; the walls that run across the hull are *bulkheads*, and the areas that are defined by them are *compartments*. The kitchen is the *galley*; the bathroom is the *head*, as is the actual toilet device in it. Windows are *portholes*, and if they can be opened they are *portlights*; if they can not be opened they are *deadlights*.

Beds (which almost certainly are convertible from and into seating) are known as *berths*. Often the spaces that extend from the interior of the cabin back out along the sides of the cockpit under the gunwales are called *quarter berths*, and they are great for dumping raingear, charts, flashlights, and everything else into, and not great at all for sleeping. The wedge-shaped compartment in the front of the boat is the *forecastle*, which is pronounced FOXull. The smaller storage area ahead of it is the *forepeak*, and it is handy for storing anchors, line, and the like. The bed that is often found in the forecastle and that, like the compartment, is shaped like a piece of pie, is the *vee-berth*, and it provides endless hours of diversion for sleepers with big feet.

Storage compartments are *lockers*; ones big enough to hang clothes in are *hanging lockers*. *Headroom* refers to vertical distance from a compartment's deck to its overhead. When a boat has *standing headroom* its main cabin has ample room for most people to stand up straight in it. Usually "standing headroom" is directly related to the height of the person who bought the boat.

At the very bottom of the interior of the boat, out of sight but never out of the proper sailor's mind, is the *bilge*, often referred to in the plural as the *bilges*. This is the place where everything (usually but not necessarily wet) that falls down ends up—water from the sea, spilled oil from an inboard engine, stray flashlight batteries, ballpoint pens. Bilges, like the trays that catch spills in the bottoms of refrigerators, have a way of getting very rank in a hurry. Material collected in the bilges disturbs the boat's balance and stability, too, and so it must be pumped out, with a *bilge pump*. Bilge is also the name for the stuff that collects in the bilges.

"Bilge" is, all on its own, a powerful word, one of those terms that has the capacity to convey to the mind of someone who doesn't even know it a pretty strong hint of what it's about. There are dozens of other sailboat terms, far prettier, that a basic list should not include, but I will throw in a handful of my favorites—words I try to use whenever I can, not to demonstrate some spurious command of the nautical vocabulary but rather for the pure joy of hearing them:

Pintles and *gudgeons* are not the senior partners of a law firm, or even the name of some British fast-food sensation, but rather the metal pins and sockets which form the hinges for removable objects such as rudders and locker doors.

Strakes are the horizontal planks that run the length of the sides of some boats. The *garboard strakes* are the planks down nearest the keel.

And my favorite: *tumblehome*. On many sailboats the topsides, which may have curved outward extravagantly at the middle of the boat, sweep inward as they approach the stern, and at the very end they form a delightful curve that pulls the whole thing quite together. This is the tumblehome.

Rising—majestically, if the designer did a good job—from the basic structure of our sailboat are the *spars*, the *sails*, and their *rigging*. It all looks very confusing at first, but a little time spent figuring out what work each one does will help marvelously to untangle the situation.

Spars include *masts* and *booms* and other devices which we won't go into here, such as *gaffs* and *boomkins*. Our basic sailing sloop will probably have only one mast and one boom. The *mast* is vertical or nearly so (it may be *raked* on a racing sailboat, which helps to explain why so many of them look rakish). It very likely will be removable; the sailor or a boatyard will be able to *unstep* it so it'll go under low bridges or can be placed in storage and *step* it when it's back on open water. The foot of the mast is its *heel*, and its top is the *masthead*. If the mast ever breaks, your boat will become *dismasted*, and your speed and comfort in getting home will depend largely on what sort of job you do of *jury-rigging* something to fly the sails from.

The *boom* is the horizontal spar that is connected to the mast down close to the deck (by a piece of hardware called the *gooseneck*) and that extends out toward the stern of the boat.

The sails are also known as *canvas*, although few of them are these days; most are made from synthetic fabrics that resist rotting and mildew. On the basic sloop, with its sole mast, the sail forward of the mast is the *jib*. (If, in more complicated configurations, there is more than one sail forward, it is a *headsail*.) The basic, everyday jib is a *working jib*; a larger one, big enough to overlap with the rear sail, is a *Genoa*, called *gennie* frequently by sailors; small, especially strong ones are called *storm jibs*.

Spinnakers are very large and often colorful sails that fly from the bow. They are made of very lightweight material and fill easily with air, and are used largely when the wind comes from aft. They are a pain in the neck to raise and

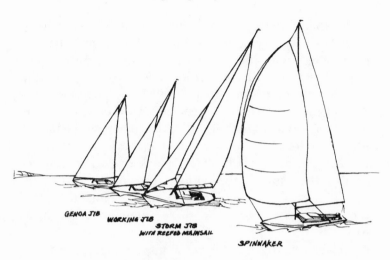

Kinds of sails

lower, and often they are seen in advertisements for ciga-
rettes, liquor, and other alleged components of the good
life. In recent years another form of lightweight, downwind
sail has invaded the market. It is a combination of spinnaker
and regular jib, with less square footage than the spinnaker
and therefore fewer headaches, and handling qualities that
are similar to a jib's. These are called *cruising spinnakers*, and
their manufacturers have given them a variety of semi-
generic, semi-proprietary names that make them sound like
reindeer: Flasher, Thrasher, and Drifter.

The *mainsail*, or *main*, is the sail that flies behind the
mast and that is held down by the boom. It, the jib, and any
other sails that belong to a particular boat are its *suit of sails*.
As might be expected, sails have a rich vocabulary of their
own. In the case of the triangular sails that go with the basic
sloop, the forward edge is called the *luff*, the after edge the
leech (sometimes spelled *leach*), and the lower edge the *foot*.
The topmost corner is the *head* of the sail, the forward
corner is the *tack*, and the after corner is the *clew*.

A Forgiving Wind

Mnemonic devices are as helpful in sailing as elsewhere, and when I was trying to learn my sail geography I had a real problem with the names of some of the corners and edges. The *foot* is obvious, as is the *head*, and after a little experimenting I realized that it would be possible to remember that the forward corner of both jib and main was the corner at which they were "tacked" down on the boat. I still have a lot of trouble with *leech* and *luff*, and until recently my mind went absolutely blank when I tried to remember the name of the bottom rear corner of the sail. Then it came to me: I couldn't remember it; I hadn't a *clew*. It embarrasses me to make these admissions, but it all works.

When you attach a sail to the mast or rigging, you are *bending* it, and when you hoist it, you *make sail*. The main is attached to its mast and boom in a variety of ways, including *slides and tracks* or a *boltrope*, which is a rope sewn into the luff or foot of the sail itself that is pushed into a track on the mast or boom. The jib is not connected to the boom; rather, its tack is affixed to the bow by a piece of hardware named the *shackle* and its luff is attached by sliding *snap hooks* onto a cable, called the *forestay*, that extends from the masthead to the bow. Another cable is used to lift the jib's head toward the masthead. The remaining corner of the jib, the clew, remains semi-free; two lines from it go to the cockpit, where the sailor can use them to control the front sail. The exact technique will be dealt with later.

When a storm comes, or when the wind builds to such force that things are getting uncomfortable and maybe a little unsafe, you *shorten sail*—literally shorten the amount of sail that's available for the wind to strike. (The methods for doing this will come up later.) And when you take the sail down in a hurry, you *dowse* it.

The sailboat's *rigging* is intimately connected with both sails and spars. Rigging may be defined as all the lines and cables that support the spars and sails, and it may be sorted into two major categories: *standing rigging*, which is connected to fixed spars and therefore stays pretty much in one place, and *running rigging*, which is used in lifting and adjusting the sails and which therefore leads a much more active life.

Standing rigging frequently is made of twisted, stranded metal cable. The cables that run from the top of the mast down to the gunwales of the boat are *shrouds*, and those that run from the masthead to the bow and stern are known as *stays*. As noted before, the stay to the bow is called the *forestay*, or, sometimes, the *headstay*. The one to the stern is the *backstay*. Many boats don't have backstays, and some are designed so that shrouds are dispensed with altogether.

Tension on the shrouds is adjusted by *turnbuckles*, and getting the adjustment just right is an art and a science. When a sailboat is moving along with a moderate degree of heel, you can see that the shrouds on the side the wind is on will be taut, while the opposite shrouds will be limber. This is a normal condition.

There may be more than one set of shrouds, and they may be connected with or run to a short crossarm that intersects the mast well toward the top. The crossarm is the *spreader*, and its purpose is to provide more bracing strength for the shrouds.

Standing rigging is confusing to the beginner, and even an experienced sailor is bewildered when he sees rigging in configurations that are unfamiliar. But if you take a moment just to stare at the cables, to note where they come from and where they end up, very often their missions will come clear.

This is an even easier task with the running rigging: the rigging that is used to control sails. This rigging is more likely to be made of rope than cable, although some of it may start out as one and end up as the other. (A word about *rope* here: You can call it anything you want to, of course, but dedicated sailors insist that, with a few exceptions, *rope* is only the thing you buy in the store. Once it is cut and assigned to some job, it becomes a *line*.)

Halyards are used to raise and lower the sails. They originate at or near the junction of the mast and the deck, and they go up to the masthead, pass through a permanent pulley, and come down again. (Halyards are likely to be among those pieces of rigging that consist of cable and rope spliced together.) One end (usually cable) is shackled to the head of the sail and the sailor hauls away at the other (usually rope) until the sail is up. Then the free end is *made fast* to something, usually a *cleat* on the mast. There is a *main halyard* and there is a *jib halyard*, and if you have your own personal flag, your *burgee*, you may want to add a halyard for raising that as well.

Sheets are the lines that are used to control the tension and direction of the sails—to pull them in and let them out. On their way toward the cockpit, they may need to make several changes in direction. Gentle turns are assisted by fixed devices, called *fairleads*, which reduce friction, while sharp changes require pulleys, which sailors know as *blocks*. Sheets may be wrapped around *winches*, which are drums that turn only one way and that provide enormous mechanical advantage so that a tiny crew member can haul in an immense Genoa that is full of wind. Sheets usually end up at *cleats*.

Cleats are variations on, and sometimes virtual replicas of, the devices that are used at home to hold the cords for bamboo blinds in place. On the boat, an ordinary *deck cleat* is similar in structure to the household item: a horizontal pin, in effect, that is raised on short legs off the deck. A line or sheet is passed around the legs, wrapped across the top of the pin in a figure-eight pattern, and given another half-wrap. The result, if the maneuver is done correctly, is a tightly secured line that will not be able to work itself loose, but that can be easily freed by the sailor. There are many variations on the basic cleat, some of them aimed at making it even easier to release a line quickly, and they have names such as *jam cleats*, *cam cleats*, and *clam cleats*.

The line that connects the *anchor* and the boat is not part of the rigging, but its importance is right up there with shrouds and sheets. An anchor (there are numerous types, with certain anchors being better for certain types of bottoms) is not connected by a rope, but rather by a *chain* or *line* or both (with the line attached to a short length of chain that is shackled to the anchor), or, in the vocabularies of some, by an *anchor rode*.

CHAPTER FIVE

The Language of Sailing

The process of actually getting out there and sailing is dependent on a special vocabulary every bit as much as is the geography of the boat itself. While there may be fewer specific objects whose names must be remembered, the need for quick and precise communication is crucially important. This can be demonstrated by a quick, typical trip out on our boat.

First of all, you really should wear *deck shoes* or their equivalent, unless the boat's owner has advised you otherwise. This is not to assure your position at the peak of preppie fashion, although I have noticed that the scruffiest of sailors can gain easy admission to nice saloons and eating places if they are wearing yellow slickers and Topsiders. There are two other, more important reasons: The specially-constructed soles will help prevent your slipping on a wet deck, and the white, rubbery material out of which the soles are constructed will not mark up the deck.

The Language of Sailing

Upon arriving at your boat (which could be *lying at anchor*, fixed to a *mooring*, or *tied up at the dock*—possibly in a *slip*) and checking the equipment, you begin to *bend on* your sails. In the case of the jib, you shackle down the tack of the sail first, then *hank on* the luff, using the built-in snaps. You do this from the bottom up, and when you get to the top of the luff, or the head of the jib, you attach the halyard. You fasten the *jib sheets* to the clew of the sail if they aren't already there, and pass them through the fairleads and blocks to the cockpit, one on each side. Depending on the sort of sail and the way the boat was designed, the sheets could go inside or outside the shrouds. At the *ends* of the sheets you tie *stop knots*, which are simple, easily-untied knots that keep a line from passing through a block or some other piece of hardware.

If the mainsail is not already attached to the boom, you fasten it now and then fix its luff to the slides or tracks that rise up the mast. The main halyard now is shackled to the head of the main. In dealing with halyards you must never let either end really get away from you, for if one does, it is likely that the lighter end of the cable will shoot up to the top of the mast and you then will be awarded the task of figuring out how to get it down again.

You are almost ready to sail. A member of your crew or you, with one of the many hands that are required at moments such as this, stands ready to *cast off* the boat from whatever's holding it. (Or, if you motored out of a harbor as we did that first time in Oriental, you reach deep water and head into the wind and prepare to kill the motor.) With halyards in place, you look *aloft* to make sure none of the rigging is tangled and that the sails are hanked on properly. It can be very embarrassing to hoist a sail and find that it will go only as far as the spreader bars because the halyard's tangled, or to find that you've put it on upside down.

A Forgiving Wind

You raise the sails, main first. The sheets that control the jib and the main will be loose and *free*, and so the sails will flap around a lot—they will *luff*, in another of those expressions that has more than one meaning. You will be *in irons*. (This is one time when you want to be in irons. Sometimes the condition imposes itself on you uninvited when you're changing course.)

By now, you will have chosen the direction you want to go—or, more likely, the conditions of wind direction and traffic around you will have dictated the choice for you. You must be aware, more than ever, of the wind now, and of which side of your boat is the *windward* side and which is the *leeward* (pronounced LOOard). The side of the boat, or of anything else, that is first touched by the breeze is the windward side; its other side is the leeward. When you anchor off an idyllic island and go ashore to bake clams and spend the night, you may choose to unroll your sleeping bag on its leeward side in order to shelter yourself from the direct wind; or, you may choose the windward side to avoid the mosquitoes. On the third hand, a sailor in a boat wants to avoid a *lee shore*. This is the shore of a body of land that is on the boat's leeward side. A boat anchoring off it or approaching it too closely may be swept against it by the wind and run aground.

You will not be heading to either left or right in your sailboat, but rather to *port* or *starboard*. Sailors have evolved a number of devices for remembering which of these is which ("port" has the same number of letters as "left," for example), and the great American free enterprise system has even sought to help matters by producing tee shirts with directions conveniently labeled on them. But I have found that if you just try to think of your left hand as your port hand, and your right as your starboard, eventually it sinks in and you find yourself actually thinking the words, rather than having to translate them from dry-land English.

With direction chosen and sails up, you use a combination of tiller action and sheet-tightening to begin your departure. If you are anchored, you *weigh anchor* and if you are at a dock or mooring you now *cast off* your lines. You are getting *under way*. But before you are able to make much progress in getting where you want to be, you must have *headway*, also called *steerageway*. This means you must have water moving past your rudder. Without that, the rudder has nothing to turn against and you are helpless to control your direction.

One way to *make headway* is to move the tiller in the direction opposite to the one you want to go, then tighten the sheet (either jib or main; if you have a crew to help, the jib is preferable) and grab the boom or jib's clew and manually pull the sail over in the same direction. This technique for catching a sailful of wind is known as *backing* the sail, and it is easier to do than to describe. What backing does is give the wind something to push against, and the pushing shoves the boat over in the opposite direction. The boat starts moving, which is what you were after. Water starts trickling, then rushing, past the rudder. The helmsman begins to feel a sort of life in the tiller. Whoever has been backing the sail can let go of it now, and the wind will push it over to the other side of the boat, but it'll still be swollen with air. The boat is pointed at a distinct angle away from the wind now; you are *falling off* the wind. You are *sailing*.

It is very important during all phases of sailing to know where the wind is coming from, but at this moment it is essential. Many sailors rely on *telltales*, which are storebought devices or bits of yarn, feather, or other lightweight material and which are fixed to the shrouds. Telltales respond quickly and easily to wind direction, and lots of sailors would feel lost without them. But often sailors *are* without them, for the necessarily flimsy pieces of fluff have a habit of disintegrating in midair.

Eventually the sailor will have to learn to judge wind direction by more lasting means, and the best way to do this is to cultivate a sensitivity for the touch of wind on your cheek, your forehead, or the back of your neck. It sounds unlikely at first, but one day it's there, and you'll never lose it.

Most of the time, wind direction is the sort of thing that doesn't need to be articulated. It's just there, and you steer and direct the boat accordingly. But changes in wind direction may require labels so they may be more conveniently stored in and retrieved from your mind, for they have a lot to do with impending changes in the weather. When the wind changes its direction in a clockwise movement (as from northeasterly to southerly, or southwesterly to northwesterly) it is said to be *veering*. If the movement is counterclockwise, the wind is *backing*. This can be easily remembered if you recall that the numbers on a compass or a clock progress in a clockwise manner, and that to reverse that progression is to go *back*wards.

Winds are named for the directions from which they come. A wind that comes out of the northwest and zips toward the southeast is a *northwesterly wind*. A wind out of the west, by the way, is called a *zephyr*.

△ △ △

You're out on open water now, with the wind on one side of your sailboat, and you're feeling strangely and ecstatically freer than you were a few minutes ago. You may or may not have a destination in mind. Either way, you're going to have to keep at the very summit of your brain your *point of sail*.

The points of sail are simply the names for the several major directions a sailboat may take and the ways its sails are adjusted for them. They are easily represented by a drawing or mental image of a circle. A compass or clock face are excellent aids here.

The wind in our representation comes out of the very top of the circle, from 12 o'clock. A boat headed generally toward 6 o'clock is *running*, or *running free*, or *sailing free*, or *before the wind*, or any number of other equally emotion-packed things. It is going *downwind*. The boom and main-sail are far out to one side to catch the wind—forming an angle of maybe 90 degrees to the centerline of the boat—and the airfoil effect is not in operation. The wind is truly pushing the boat along. Because the mainsail extends so far out to the side, it *blankets* the jib and causes it to lose its burden of air. The sailor may then choose to go *wing and wing*, which means main out on one side and jib out on the other. It is one of the prettiest forms of sailing, particularly when a large, colorful, spinnaker-type jib is used. The boat scoots along on these runs, pushed by both wind and wind-driven waves. The boat does not heel, and there is a general air of relaxation.

As handsome and restful as downwind sailing may be, it presents a constant danger of an unexpected jibe. That, you may recall, occurs when the wind gets on the wrong side of the boom and slaps it across the boat with tremen-dous force, cracking everything in its way (including the crew's heads) and in extreme cases cracking the mast as well. (Deliberate jibing will be discussed a little later.)

If the boat is aiming somewhat to the left or right of 6 o'clock—say, around 4 or 8 o'clock—it is on a *broad reach*. The sails are pulled in a bit, to about three-quarters of their

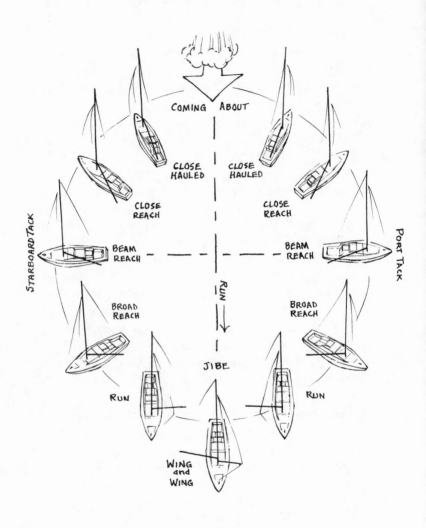

The points of sail

angle when the boat was running. The wind is still pretty much to the aft of the boat, but it comes only from one side and there is much less danger of its getting around the boom and causing an unintentional jibe.

Now the boat is at a right angle to the wind, at 3 or 9 o'clock, and it is sailing on a *beam reach*. The mainsail and boom form about a 45 degree angle with the boat's center-line. This is a safe and generally comfortable point of sail, with no danger of a jibe and only a moderate amount of heeling. It was well after my first experience at Oriental that I started to learn the points of sail and realized that when Mary had handed me the tiller, I had gravitated very quickly to the beam reach.

As we head up the clock face now, toward the direction from which the wind is coming, we are starting to sail *upwind*. The action—wind, spray, our degree of heel, the noise—starts to pick up, and we have the feeling that we are traveling faster. (We may not be. The increased excitement often just makes us think we've speeded up.) The main is sheeted in close to the center of the boat, and when it's about a quarter of the way out and our direction is around 2 or 10 o'clock on the imaginary circle, we may be said to be on a *close reach*.

We sail even closer to the wind—which is to say, we continue *pointing*, or *pointing up*, the ultimate *point* being the wind's own direction. But we will not be able to sail when we are dead into the wind: remember what happens when that occurs? The wind is unable to fill either side of the sails, they luff and flap about, and forward motion ceases. Many sailboats cannot get closer than 45 degrees, on either side, to the top of our imaginary circle without falling in irons. When they are about as close as practicable, they are sailing *close-hauled* (the sails are hauled in close); they are *beating* or *on a beat*.

Once we have learned the points of sail and how to achieve them, we have automatically learned a good deal about how to *change course*. If our boat is running downwind—say, it is headed due east, with a westerly wind almost directly behind it—and its mainsail is flying well out to port, and we want to change our course and head due south, our task is an easy one. We merely push the tiller away from us (if we're sitting on the starboard side), toward port, and the rudder will cause the boat to curve around to starboard. At the same time, we haul in a bit on the main sheet and make adjustments to the jib, and we find ourselves on a broad reach, headed toward the southeast. Continue the maneuvering with the tiller and sheets and we'll be on a beam reach, headed pretty much due south. By continuing these actions, which are called *hardening up*, or *coming up*, we can curve farther around to the southwest, but we will not be able to effect a complete reversal of our course and sail off directly into the west, since that's where the wind is coming from. (If our positions were reversed, and we wanted to change from sailing close-hauled to running, our tiller and sheet work would be reversed and we would be *falling off* the wind; *heading down*.)

All our mobility in that little experiment, we note, has been confined to one-half of the clock face of our imaginary circle. In this instance it was the area between about 7 o'clock and about 10:30, but it just as easily could have been the arc between about 5 o'clock and 1:30. What happens if we want to make changes in direction that require our crossing from one of the halves of the circle to the other—that require that we radically alter our relationship to the wind so that it starts striking us on the opposite side of the boat?

Suppose, for example, that we're on a broad reach to the southeast (at 7:30 o'clock), the wind is coming from the west (12 o'clock), and we want to set out toward the north (3 o'clock). Or suppose we're sailing close-hauled toward the southwest (10 o'clock) and we want to change course to the northwest (2 o'clock). In sailing, we must make choices such as these all the time, for there is no end to the obstacles—rocks, beaches, other boats, continents—that are constantly requiring us to change our course.

If we are sailing upwind, we will have to change course repeatedly, in a zig-zag fashion, to get where we're headed if the place we're headed for lies directly in the wind. If we are on a *collision course* with another boat, one of us will have to change course. (Which one of us must do that is carefully prescribed in the nautical *rules of the road*, the compendium of regulations that govern marine traffic similar to the way a body of laws and customs applies to auto travel, but, as often is the case in terrestrial rules of the road, the other guy often doesn't obey them and you must be prepared to do all the work yourself.) If an object is *dead ahead* of us, we will have to change course to avoid it by a comfortable margin, to *give it a wide berth*. So what do we do in all these situations?

We reach into our bag of many-faceted sailing words and *tack*. In this case, the term pertains to two slightly different situations. It refers to the course a boat is taking in relationship to the wind; a sailboat is on a *port tack* if the wind is striking it from the port side and causing the boom to be on the starboard side; in a *starboard tack* the opposite conditions prevail. (This is a legal definition, for it is used in the rules of the road to determine which boats in given situations have right-of-way.) A sailboat that is moving through the water is always on one tack or the other, or it is in the process of changing from one tack to the other.

Tacking also refers to the act of changing from one tack to the other, and that is what happens when you alter your course in front of the wind, as in the examples cited above.

Since the course changes discussed earlier did not involve shifting the boat's boom from one side to the other, they were not tacks. A further sub-category of this definition of tacking is the zig-zag course you follow when you tack back and forth to get to a destination. You say, "We had a fine run down there, but we had to tack all the way home."

A downwind tack is called a *jibe* (sometimes spelled "gybe") and, since it is a course change that the sailor plans for, it lacks the danger and hysteria that often accompany unplanned jibes. Consider the imaginary clock face again: The boat is on that broad reach toward the southeast, at 7:30 on the clock. The skipper wants to go toward the north. He warns his crew and passengers of the impending course change: *"Prepare to jibe."* Skipper or crew use the main sheet to haul the boom in most of the way from its position far out on the port side of the boat. The skipper smoothly pushes the tiller to starboard so that the boat will turn to port. Before the boat crosses in front of the wind, the skipper shouts, *"Jibe ho!"* There will be an instant at which the wind stops filling the mainsail on its starboard side and starts filling it on the port side. The speed and force with which this change can occur are major reasons why all jibes should be carefully planned and executed. The sail fills quickly—very quickly if there's a lot of wind—and the boat is sailing on a new tack (in this case the port tack). It has crossed the half of the clock face and now may continue, on the new tack, its alteration of course to point it up toward the north.

Pandemonium during planned jibes can be kept to a minimum by hauling in the mainsheet at the beginning so that the boom has very little distance to travel when the jibe occurs, and by letting the sheet out rather quickly once the sail starts to fill again on the new tack. This last helps keep the wind from exerting a great deal of force against the sail and boat and causing severe heeling. In a boat without a weighted keel, it is necessary for the passengers and skipper to shift their weight to the new windward side to balance the boat. The jib requires little attention during the jibe itself, and may be repositioned and trimmed once the boom has crossed the cockpit.

An upwind tack is referred to as *coming about*, or, by some people, as simply a *tack* (they refer to the downwind change only as a *jibe*). It is considerably less exciting than the jibe, since the boom swings across the deck with much less assertiveness.

Suppose our sailboat is headed close-hauled on a port tack toward 2 o'clock on the imaginary clock face, and we want to change course and head down toward 10 o'clock. The wind is coming from 12 o'clock. We could get where we are going by falling off from our close-hauled course to a close reach, then through a beam reach, broad reach, and run; then we could jibe and approach 10 o'clock from the other side of the clock, all of which would take time and would mean we would have to sail temporarily away from the direction we were heading. Or we could change our course by coming about.

We point the sailboat up until it is close-hauled and sailing as close to the wind as possible. Then, as the skipper announces, *"Stand by to come about,"* or delivers some equivalent warning, the crew uncleats the jib sheet from its position on the starboard side of the boat and holds the sheet fast, by hand, while the skipper pushes the tiller to starboard and shouts, *"Hard alee!"* or *"Helm's alee!"* This indicates that she is turning the rudder toward the lee side of the boat, and so it signals an abrupt change of course.

The boat moves toward the wind. For a moment we are in irons, but it is only for a moment, as the boat's forward motion carries us past the point where we are aiming dead into the wind. The wind starts striking the boat from just the other side of its bow. The crew (or skipper, if this is a *singlehanded* cruise) waits until precisely the right moment and then loosens the "old" jib sheet (in this case the starboard one) and hauls in on the "new" sheet. The jib snaps across the deck, and as it is filling with air the crew is hauling in on the port sheet and securing it. Now the jib is full of air, and it and the skipper's touch on the tiller carry the boat through the turn. Almost unnoticed in all this is the fact that the mainsail and boom, which had been in close-hauled position on the port tack, have swung uneventfully the short distance across the deck and are now in the corresponding position on the starboard tack. The boat is now sailing on the other side of the wind, and the skipper sets about adjusting and fine-tuning the course to get where she wants to go.

As much as anything else in sailing, the perfection of tacking and jibing techniques depends on repetition and experience. There are some occasions when the sailor chooses not to jibe—fearing that too much wind would slam the boom across too severely even in a planned maneuver—and then the downwind course change can be accomplished by coming about.

Instead of jibing, the skipper just hardens up—from runs to reaches to close-hauled—and then comes about and falls off in the other direction until he is on the desired course. This may sound like a big loss of time and effort, but the curlique that is described by the boat can be a very small one, owing to the fact that the wind is helping to turn the boat rather quickly.

△ △ △

As our sail continues, we spend a good portion of our time adjusting the sails, trying to get the best possible uses out of the wind and the boat's equipment. We are *trimming* the sails. Here, as elsewhere, we find one word with more than one meaning: *Trimming* is used to mean adjusting in general, but it also refers specifically to tightening the sheets. Its opposite expression is *easing*. We are guided in these adjustments by looking at the sails themselves and seeing how they are faring in the wind as we cut through the water. One test for sail trim involves yet another double meaning. You watch the luff of your jib and ease the sheet until it begins to luff—in other words, you watch the sail's leading edge and loosen the sheet until the leading edge starts to flap—and then you trim the sheet until just past the point where the luff disappears.

Wind conditions, or the conditions of wind in combination with waves, may become such that you feel it necessary to adjust your sails drastically—to *shorten sail*. If you're moving along on a close reach and the wind builds to such force that your boat is heeled over uncomfortably far, you can reduce the amount of sail that the wind has to play with by shortening it. Shortening sail is the generic name for a number of measures that may be taken to reduce sail area. One of them is called *reefing* or *taking a reef*. It involves using whatever method your boat and sails are equipped for to reduce the area of the main (or, in some cases, the jib) with relative ease. On the Ensign in Lake Walloon, the main halyard could be eased and the mainsail lowered a few feet and the slack taken up by revolving the boom and wrapping the excess sail around it. Other boats have special *reef points*, which are lines sewn into the lower part of the sail, parallel with the foot, that may be used to tie the slack down around the boom.

The area of the jib may be shortened by switching to a smaller sail—from Genoa to working sail, for instance. The ultimate sail-shortening maneuver consists of taking the sails down altogether. Or, in a heavy blow you may decide to *heave to*. This means doing everything you can (with sails up) to keep the boat pointed directly into the wind and therefore minimally at its mercy.

△ △ △

As we return from our sail, we face the inevitable task of coming to a stop—of *anchoring*, or tying up at our *mooring*, or of coming into the *dock*. If there is one constant about sailing, it is that sooner or later, sailors must renew their relationship with dry land.

The coming-to-a-halt maneuvers are all similar, with notable variations. They all require that the sailor maneuver the boat in such a way that it comes to a stop at pretty much the point where he wants it to. This is done relatively easily with the sails down and the engine on, and reverse thrust on the motor's propeller blades comes in very handy at such moments. But for the sailor confined to wind power, stopping and tying up mean depriving the boat of the force that's been driving it along all day, and depriving it at just the right moment. As you can well imagine, experience and repetition work wonders here.

Anchor is both verb and noun. It refers to the metal device (also known as *ground tackle*) that helps the boat cling to the bottom and stay in one place, and to the act of putting the device down (also known as *dropping the hook*). The sailor sails his boat into the wind (*luffs up*) so that it comes to a stop perhaps three boatlengths upwind of the place where he'd like for it to end up. Someone drops the anchor—does not throw it, however tempted to do so, for throwing it increases the likelihood of tangling the anchor line (*fouling it*)—and *pays out* the line until the anchor strikes the bottom.

Because anchors and their lines must be available for duty at either end of the boat and for other reasons, often the anchor is stowed someplace until it's needed and the free end of the line is not ordinarily tied to anything. This is the *bitter end*. Consequently, before the sailor or crew drops the hook, he must make sure that the bitter end is fastened to something strong—a cleat on the deck set for the purpose, or even the foot of the mast. It is equally important to make sure that the anchor line is not wrapped around your own foot or leg or anything else that you'd rather not see swept hurriedly off the deck and into the water.

With the anchor on the bottom, the sailor pays out more line. The amount depends on several factors, including the length of the intended stay at anchor and the intensity of the wind, current, and wave action. A generally accepted minimum amount is three times the estimated depth of the water. The maximum is. perhaps seven times the water depth. This whole business is known as *scope*: insuring that the angle that the anchor line makes with the bottom is sufficiently small that the anchor will have good holding power. An anchor connected to a boat that is directly above it will have very little holding power. It will be likely to *drag*. But one tied to a boat that rocks on the surface many feet away will be able to dig its horns, or *flukes*, into the bottom with much greater efficiency.

Now, with the proper amount of scope out and the boat drifted back to the point downwind where the skipper wanted to stop, the crew gives the line a half-turn around the heavy cleat at the bow of the boat. This handy little maneuver is called *snubbing* the line; it enables the crew member to stop the boat's backward drift almost effortlessly by transferring the strain to the cleat. Just holding on to the line could be an arm-wrenching (or even unexpected-swimming) experience. Snubbing is used in a number of other shipboard situations, as well. If all is going well, the anchor will be dug into the bottom and the crew can fix the anchor line more permanently in place, and lower the sails.

A Forgiving Wind

Leaving an anchorage, or *weighing anchor*, is pretty much the reverse of the above procedure.

If your destination is a *mooring*, a float that rides the surface and is connected by rope or chain to a permanent anchor at the bottom, you approach in the same manner, except that instead of dropping the anchor when you come to a halt you reach over the side and shackle a line from the bow to an eye in the float.

In docking, as in anchoring and mooring, the object is to run out of wind at just the right time so you are where you want to be and can reach over and make fast your *dock lines* to the dock's cleats or pilings.

Coming in to a dock generally means a limited number of options as to direction from which you may approach, since half the dock is against the land and therefore off limits for the boat. There can be other complications: If you come in to a mooring a little too hot, little harm will be done if you run past it or even give it a thump; you go around and do it again. But ramming a dock is considered bad form by just about everybody. Also, there are other boats at docks, and the space you have to get into may seem perilously small and way too close to someone's $40,000 dream yacht.

Docks present a further hazard, known to the sailing community as the *dock committee*. This refers to the person or persons who suddenly materialize on the dock as you approach it. These people stand there, watching the moves you make and (you are quite certain) harshly judging the way you're making them. It is painfully obvious that they think you're a rotten sailor. The very skilled ones will back away from where they're standing as you make your final approach, as if to signal that they fully expect you to demolish the dock. It is likely that half of them are not sailors at all, and that half the rest aren't even as skilled as you are. But that is not the point. The point is that they are

Flemished line

your hypercritical, cruel audience at the very moment when you desire complete, total anonymity.

You arrive at the dock anyway, and the world does not come to an end. The dock committee shuffles off to stare some other sailor into hysteria, and you coil up your lines and stow your sails and start remembering how fine sailing is. It is emotionally satisfying at moments such as this to *flemish* your lines. This means forming loose ends of line into flatly-coiled circles on the deck, like in movies about the golden age of sailing. Flemished lines are no more essential to sailing than sailing is essential to water transportation. But both are extremely handsome, and that's part of what sailing is all about.

CHAPTER SIX

Triangles and Protractors

Not long after the beginning sailor has learned a touch of the language and a working knowledge of the points of sail and how to execute them, the time comes when he or she must decide where to go with that knowledge.

It may be that sailing occupies a pleasurable but tiny portion of his life, and that it is sufficient to rent a Sunfish once or twice a summer and to tack gracefully back and forth on sunny vacation afternoons. Or it may turn out that the beginner, having gulped a mouthful of wind-driven spray, finds he has a well-nigh insatiable appetite for sailing; that he is inexplicably addicted to it; that it has transcended the levels of "fun" and "therapy" and "relaxation" and has insinuated itself into the center of his life. I suspect that this is the case with a good many people who enjoy sailboat racing. And it could be the motivation that drives those whose permanent homes are their boats, the *live-aboards*.

Or it may be (as it is in my own case) that the fascination with sailing produces feelings that are somewhere in between: The sailor knows he cannot assign his whole life to sailing, the need to make a living being what it is, but he knows also that a portion of his life must be reserved for sailing, learning about sailing, planning sailing, fantasizing about sailing. This sort of sailor knows that if an undefined but very certain period of time goes by during which he has *not* been sailing, he will become sad and feel that something important is missing from his life.

People in this category are well represented in all forms of sailing, from board boaters to ocean competitors, but they seem to be especially prevalent among the *cruising sailors*. These are the sailing equivalent of backpackers. They are the sailors who go out into nature with the aims of enjoying her and coexisting with her, but not challenging or plundering her. They want to be self-sustaining, yet to do as little damage as possible.

If "where to go" for the beginning sailor is any of the above, other than the simplest sort of darting about on millponds, it becomes essential that the sailor learn a little *navigation*. "Essential" implies some sort of mandatory requirement that the sailor absorb this category of the nuts and bolts of sailing, and that may be misleading. Navigation is not something that is studied and memorized in the classroom and then tested out on the water. A sailor's learning of the map of the water is as natural and voluntary as the walker's learning the map of the land. And, just as the hiker who can navigate her way through the mountains gets positive benefits from knowing what is where, where the streams and springs and good views are and where the trails start and end and intersect, so the sailor who knows how to get where she's going will learn to see and enjoy more— and, in an important added attraction, will be better able to avoid danger and the discomforts of running aground.

Navigation has its own list of terms and definitions,

starting with *navigation* itself. Elbert S. Maloney, in the thirteenth edition to his nautical classic, *Dutton's Navigation & Piloting* (Annapolis: Naval Institute Press, 1978), writes that navigation "is the process of directing the movement of a vehicle from one point to another," and adds that "To make the definition complete, the qualification of 'safely' or 'successfully' should be added." Maloney and other students of the subject always note that both art and science are involved in navigation, particularly the sort of navigation that is both safe and successful.

One very old and very reverend method for directing a boat's movement utilizes the predicted and observed positions of astronomical bodies, along with the sailor's knowledge of mathematical formulas and of the precise time of day. This is called *celestial navigation*, and it is far beyond the scope of this book (although there will be a brief exploration of it later on). Celestial navigation is rarely used in coastal and inland waters. The favored form of navigation there is called *piloting*, which means getting where you're going by referring to visible, close-by objects, such as buoys and other markers in the water, the depth of the water itself, and landmarks on the shore. These devices which assist the navigator are all *navigational aids*. (Purists disagree on the precise definition. They insist that *aids to navigation* include only manmade objects outside the boat but on the water—buoys, beacons, and so forth—that assist navigation, while *navigational aids* also include charts and instruments on the boat.)

Dead reckoning is a component of piloting that involves using known information, such as your starting-out position according to the location of buoys or landmarks, your speed, and the distance you've traveled, to predict where you are. A position estimated by this method is a *dead reckoning position*. None of this has to do with mortality; the name comes from "ded" (for deduced) reckoning.

The boat's position at any given moment is a central part of what navigation is all about, as is its *course*—the direction in which you're traveling. And this naturally brings us to our *compass*, the device that is essential to all forms of navigation. The compass is a symbolic representation of the circle of the earth, divided into 360 equal segments called *degrees* (or °), with every tenth or so segment named—0°, 10°, 20°, 30° . . . 180°, 190°, and so on. Four of the points of the compass are named for the four basic directions—North at 0° (which is also 360°), East at 90°, South halfway around the circle at 180°, and West at 270°. The compass *card* on which this information is printed is made so that it will swing freely about its center point, and it is magnetized so that its top, at 0°, points to Earth's magnetic top. This doesn't exactly mean the North Pole, since the magnetic north is some distance away from the Pole, as far south as Thule, Greenland, and since it has a tendency to move around. A serious sailing boat has a compass mounted permanently in its cockpit, and quite likely another, hand-held one available. At the head of the transparent compass enclosure is an index mark, called the *lubber's line*, which represents the centerline of the boat. Since the compass card will always point to magnetic north, no matter which way the boat is pointed, the sailor can use the number on the card that's closest to the lubber's line as a reference point for figuring direction.

If, for example, the boat is headed down a body of water and the sailor wants to check (or confirm) her course, and the number opposite the lubber's line is 85, that means that the boat is sailing on a line that is 85 degrees clockwise from magnetic north. This could be confirmed by checking the compass card to see where North, or 0°, is. It will be pointing over toward the port side of the boat. Since 85° is very close to 90°, and since 90° is due East, the sailor might be satisfied with the general information that she is heading east. If she wants to be precise, she will say the direction is 085°, using the zero to avoid possible confusion. In either case, that is the *heading* of the boat.

The compass is useful in establishing reference points to other objects, too. Suppose our boat is on that heading of 85°, and we have been watching for a lighthouse somewhere over on the starboard side of the boat. (We have reason to believe the lighthouse is there because our chart says one is there.) A particularly sharp-eyed member of the crew spots the lighthouse, and the skipper says, "Where is it? I don't see it."

"It's at about 100°," replies the crew member. The skipper can then line her eye up with the compass, extend her gaze out past the 100° mark on the card, and have a rough idea of where the lighthouse is or where it will soon appear to her eyes. Even greater accuracy can be achieved with a *hand-bearing compass*, which is held directly in front of the eye and which may use optical devices to minimize error. When the position of the lighthouse or any other object is confirmed, its angular direction from the boat (in this case, 100°) is called its *bearing*. Several bearings may be combined to determine the place on the water where the boat is. This point is called a *fix*, and its precision is variable.

Courses, bearings, and headings may be expressed in several ways, and most of the confusion among them may be attributed to the fact that geographic north is almost never the same thing as magnetic north. A *true* heading or bearing refers to the angle stated in terms of "true" north, the one at the North Pole where Santa Claus lives. A *magnetic* heading is based on an angle stated in terms of magnetic north. The difference between the two, which varies depending on where in the world you are, is called *variation*. Because its compass responds only to magnetic north, a boat's *compass course* is its magnetic course—its heading—

but that, too, may be subject to adjustment for what is called *deviation*, which is the sum of all the local magnetic influences on board (radios, tools, soup cans, and the like). And *relative bearings* are bearings measured between the boat's heading and an object, calculated clockwise around the compass. Our lighthouse has a *bearing* of 100° (the angle between it and magnetic north, as measured from the boat), but it has a *relative bearing* of 15° (the angle between it and the boat's heading of 85°).

Latitude and *longitude* are marvelous devices for fixing, recording, and conveying information about the position of objects—cities, lighthouses, boats—on the surface of Earth. Using the imaginary lines and their almost infinite subdivisions, one creates imaginary grids on which anything can be located and its position established and communicated to others. *Longitude* lines run north and south, starting at a zero designation called the *prime meridian* which runs through Greenwich, England, and they are not parallel, since they all meet at the poles. Lines of *latitude* are parallel, to the line designated 0° at the Equator.

In the case of latitude, measurement is reckoned in degrees north and south of the Equator, with the poles at 90° North and South, respectively. Longitude is measured in degrees east and west of Greenwich, with the dividing line at 180°, in the middle of the Pacific Ocean. Degrees are divided into *minutes*, with sixty minutes to a degree, and minutes are further broken into tenths of minutes (or, by some practitioners, into *seconds*).

Thus San Francisco is at 37°45′ North (37 degrees and 45 minutes north of the Equator), 122°26′ West (122 degrees, 26 minutes west of Greenwich), and it will stay there at least until the next major earthquake. My home is a few feet north of the junction of 40°41′ North, 74°00′ West. Our imaginary boat may be at 41°02.5′ North, 73°24.3′ West. Latitude and longitude are used mainly in deep-water sailing, however, and the coastal and inland sailor may wish to employ less abstract terms. In this case, we would say our boat is in Long Island Sound, about three and a half miles south of South Norwalk, Connecticut. If we want a greater degree of precision, while continuing to avoid latitude and longitude, we can add the information that we are sailing near the abandoned lighthouse at Sheffield Island, which is one of the Norwalk Islands. Then anyone with a knowledge of the area or access to a detailed chart will be able to pinpoint our position quickly and easily.

Our boat's speed through the water, along with its anticipated speed, are helpful in navigation and in planning where we're going and when we're going to get there. Speed in sailing is measured in *knots*, which are *nautical miles* per hour. (The "per hour" is understood. You say, "We're making three knots," not "three knots an hour.") A nautical mile is longer than a statute mile, being 6,076.11549 U.S. feet as opposed to the statute mile's 5,280 feet. Statute miles may be converted into nautical miles by multiplying them by 1.15, and the reverse may be accomplished by multiplying nautical miles by 0.87.

The movement of the water we're sailing on, both vertically and horizontally, affects our navigation. On lakes, such motion is likely to be created only by the action of the wind and only on the water surface, while on larger bodies of water such as seas and ocean waters, *tide* and *current* become important factors. *Tide*, when the term is used correctly, refers strictly to the upward-and-downward movement of the water level as a result of the gravitational forces exerted by sun and moon. *Current* is the name for horizontal water motion. A current can be produced by the water flowing down a river, or it can be created by the rise-and-

fall action of the tide, in which case it is referred to as the
tidal current. Regardless of what does or does not constitute
correct usage, several million people per day persist in saying things like, "The tide's coming in now," and, "That
sure is a strong tide this morning."

When the tide is rising along a particular shoreline, the
current may be expected to be flowing from the sea toward
the shore. Later, when the tide falls, the direction of the
current will be reversed. While winds are named for the
directions from which they come, currents are identified by
the directions they're going. The speed with which a current moves, usually expressed in knots, is its *drift*, and its
direction is called its *set*. So a current that moves at two
knots from due west to due east is identified as having a
drift of two knots and a set of 90°, or, less formally, "It sets
east." Great quantities of data on tides and currents have
been assembled, and it is possible to predict with some
accuracy what water conditions will be like on a given hour
of a given day well off in the future.

Data have been collected, too, on another important bit
of navigational information: the depth of the water. Depths
are marked on navigational charts, and the charts always
specify the unit of measure, be it foot, meter, or fathom. A
fathom is six feet.

These statistics are presented in a variety of references
that are available to the sailor, some privately published and
many put out by the government. They include *tide tables*;
tidal current tables; *tidal current charts*, which depict current
movement graphically; *light lists*, which name and describe
all the characteristics of lighted aids to navigation; the *Notice
to Mariners*, which furnishes continually updated information on the condition of waterways; and the *U.S. Coast Pilot*
series, which describes piloting conditions, regulations, anchorages, land accommodations and much more along the
nation's navigable waters. Private publishers put out de-

tailed guides to specific regions of waterways, with emphasis on the commercial services that are available. And the National Oceanic and Atmospheric Administration (N.O.A.A.), which is part of the U.S. Department of Commerce, operates dozens of very high frequency broadcasting *weather radio* stations that give taped weather information twenty-four hours a day.

△ △ △

The sailor's most valued publication, however, is not a volume of printed words but rather a collection of symbols: the *nautical chart*. The chart is his ticket to the water, his insurance policy that promises the safest possible passage from one point to another. Without a chart, the skipper who is sailing into a stretch of water for the first time is virtually helpless, ignorant of exactly where his destination may be, of what might make a good port of refuge in a storm, of what the bottom is like, and of how close the bottom is to the top. With a chart (and a large dose of common sense, for charts can be wrong), the sailor has a powerful ally and protector. Even those who sail the same waters over and over again, and who may be said to know it like the backs of their hands, keep charts nearby for use on those occasions when they forget what the backs of their hands look like. And when nautical charts become outdated, they make beautiful wall decorations.

Charts come in all shapes and sizes and formats, but the ones that the sailor in the United States is likely to encounter are published by the National Ocean Survey, which is part of N.O.A.A. These charts (they are not called "maps" when they're used for boating) come in different configurations, according to the uses to which they are likely to be put. One important difference is in the *scale* of the charts, a term which sometimes can lead to confusion. Scale is expressed as a ratio, which is always printed somewhere on the chart. A scale of 1:40,000, for example, means that one unit of measure on the chart (an inch, centimeters, or whatever) represents 40,000 of the same unit out in the real world. A scale of 1:150,000 means one inch on the chart represents 150,000 inches in reality. If you had a piece of paper that was thirty-five miles wide and fifty miles long, you could draw a map of Rhode Island on it at a scale of 1:1.

Unfortunately for the sailor who tries to keep an orderly mind, the 1:150,000 scale chart is a somewhat *small scale* chart, while the 1:40,000 representation is relatively *large scale*. The reason is that the people who thought all this up decided scale was a characteristic of the fraction represented by the ratio. The fraction 1/150,000 (which is the same as the ratio 1:150,000) is smaller than the fraction 1/40,000, and so it is said to produce a smaller scale. The only possible reason for remembering any of this is that the time may come when you walk into a chart store and ask for a chart of Such-and-such area, and the clerk hands you one, and you say, "Do you have it in a larger (or smaller) scale?" Career chart store employees know the correct way to express scale, and they can be as relentless as any dock committee in persecuting the poor devil who walks in and asks the wrong question.

In any event, a chart's scale is important in the way it'll be used. Really small scale charts (1:600,000 or smaller) are used in approaching the mainland after an ocean crossing, but they would be of little use for getting into the harbor once the mainland was reached. In providing the navigator with the big picture they trade off much of the detail. Larger scale charts (those in the 1:50,000-and-up range) are most useful in entering harbors, sailing in the Great Lakes, and doing the sort of piloting that we've been discussing here.

To find out which charts are available for a given area of the United States, and in what scale, you need to consult one of the *Nautical Chart Catalogs* published by the government. These catalogs, which are actually very small scale outline maps themselves, show graphically which charts (indexed by number and title) cover which areas. There are four such catalogs, and they cover the Atlantic and Gulf Coasts, including Puerto Rico and the Virgin Islands; the Pacific Coast; Alaska and the Aleutians; and the Great Lakes and nearby bodies of water.

Nautical charts are literally covered with numbers, letters, and symbols, to a degree much greater than that which the hiker finds on a topographical map of dry land, and many of the symbols and abbreviations may not be readily comprehensible. The key to it all may be found in N.O.A.A.'s *Chart No. 1: Nautical Chart Symbols and Abbreviations*, which is not a chart at all but rather a twenty-page booklet. With *Chart No. 1*, you quickly understand the nuts and bolts of the chart: the unique symbols for a "cliffy coast," a bayou, a submerged jetty, an oyster bed, snags and stumps, rocks that are submerged, not submerged, and only sometimes submerged, and dozens of others. There are the all-important *soundings*, which are the records of water depth, expressed in the units specified on the chart. (Some, perhaps most, sailors assume that the soundings represent the lowest possible water levels, and that a boat drawing, for example, four feet will have no difficulty passing over the bottom at a place where the chart records depth as five feet. They could be in for a surprise. Charts generally report depth at *mean low water* or *m.l.w.*, and that is near the average of all the low tides at a given point, not the lowest possible tide. Just as it is possible to say that half of the people in the nation have IQs below 100—since 100 is said to be near the average—it is proper to say that half of the low tides at a particular point on a chart that records depth as "12" produce water depths of less than twelve feet.)

Charts report, and *Chart No. 1* explains, the quality and consistency of the bottom (helpful if you're in danger of running aground or if you've already done so and are considering the best way to get unstuck; mud and sand are infinitely preferable to boulders and stumps), and they provide, far better than do topographical maps, assistance in determining direction, both true and magnetic. They achieve this by means of compass diagrams, called *roses*, that are printed at several places on the chart. And charts provide information on the nature and exact position of objects on nearby land—prominent landmarks such as church steeples, water towers, bridges, and cupolas—that may be helpful to the sailor in establishing position. Perhaps most important, nautical charts depict the manmade devices that are put in and on the water itself for the purpose of telling the mariner where he is and warning him away from danger. These are the indispensable objects that the purists refer to as aids to navigation.

They include *buoys* and *beacons*, which may float on the water surface and are tethered to the bottom by chains and heavy anchors, and which come in characteristic shapes and colors. Some are called, and look like, *cans*, while others are *nuns*, after their cone-shaped tops that resemble the nuns' headgear called coifs.

Then there are *lights*, which burn continuously or display off-on patterns in red, green, or white. Each light's characteristics are different from those of any other light in the vicinity, and so a sailor who observes one, and knows where it should be and what its identifying qualities are (as he will, if he has a chart), will be able to determine his own position in relationship to the light. This category of aids includes *lighthouses*, of which there are still some spectacular ones on the American seacoasts and Great Lakes.

Contrary to what one may infer from their name, *day-beacons* are unlighted devices. They are like highway traffic signs, with characteristic shapes, colors, and numbers or letters that make them, like the lights, unique among their nearby colleagues. Daybeacons are fixed in place, usually on pilings, and thus are seen more often in shallower waters, particularly at the entrances to channels and harbors.

Ranges are sets of aids, lighted or unlighted, that are situated apart from each other in such a way that when they line up in the skipper's eye, they show him that he is in the right place. This usually means in the middle of a channel. *Radio*, *radar*, and other *electronic stations* are sometimes made part of visible buoys, lights, and beacons and provide an extra means of identification for boats that are equipped to receive their signals. And *fog signals* employ horns, whistles, bells, and gongs to create noise, sometimes by ingenious use of the motion of the waves or the rise and fall of the tide.

These aids to navigation are regulated and maintained, by and large, by the government. In most waters that are subject to federal jurisdiction, the Coast Guard is in charge and it does a commendable job. State governments may be responsible on inland waters. And on small bodies of water, lesser political jurisdictions and private groups or individuals may maintain the aids, with the result sometimes being buoys that are made out of one-gallon bleach bottles and daybeacons that are little more than dead saplings stuck into the muddy bottom. All of them, fancy or crude, serve the same purpose, though: to help the sailor determine where he is and to keep him out of trouble.

Aids to navigation are great confidence-builders. Whether you're quite sure of where you are, or have begun to feel a little uncertain, spotting a daybeacon that is bright green and has the number "21" on it, at the place where a green "21" is supposed to be, can do wonders for morale and self-assurance. With the chart and a knowledge of what

PORT SIDE (RETURNING FROM SEA)

9	**7**	**1**	**3**	**5**
BLACK/WHITE LIGHTED BUOY	BLACK CAN	GREEN/GREEN DAYMARK	GREEN/WHITE DAYMARK	GREEN/GREEN DAYMARK

STARBOARD SIDE (RETURNING FROM SEA)

4	**6**	**8**
RED/ORANGE DAYMARK	RED NUN	RED/WHITE LIGHTED BUOY

Aids to navigation

to look for, a sailor can be pretty sure of his position, even in the most unfamiliar territory or on the darkest of nights. It is important to remember, too, that things change. Charts get updated, buoys get sunk, daybeacons get damaged, and light batteries run down. Common sense is as important in navigation as it is elsewhere in sailing and other aspects of living.

CHAPTER SEVEN

Using the Navigator's Tools

All that remains for the sailor to do now is to put together the tools and devices and aids of navigation and become a navigator. Essential to that are two things: learning the language of the buoys, beacons, and lights, and learning how to plan a voyage. The most essential element of them all, experience, can only come later.

Much of the wisdom of the buoys is contained in that lesson that Mary Denmark taught me on the first day I sailed: *Red right returning*. When "returning" or passing from a larger body of water to a smaller one, as when returning from sea, the sailor keeps the red markers or lights on her right-hand side. The other markers, which generally will be black or green, or green lights, will end up on her left side. (Lights on either side can be white.) The red-green rule is reversed when going in the opposite direction. For a boat sailing along the United States coast, the "returning" route is deemed to be the clockwise direction, so a boat bound from Norfolk to Houston or one headed from San Diego to Seattle would keep the reds on her right. On the Great Lakes, "returning" means going from the outlet end to the higher end.

Colors are not the only clues. Even-numbered markers are on the right side of channels when returning, and odd-numbered ones are on the left. In the case of buoys, nuns are on the right and cans on the left. And triangular day-beacons may be found on the right and square ones on the left. Markers in other shapes and color schemes serve to identify obstructions, channel junctions, fish nets, anchorages, and a number of other things. Some even display the mileage to the next port of call.

In the case of a light, a wealth of information may be found in its pattern. It can burn constantly, or it can flash at an ordinary rate, can be a quick flasher, can send out interrupted flashes, and can even send Morse code. All of this serves to identify the light, to render it separate from all other lights that are nearby.

Translating one's knowledge of navigation to the chart, with the aim of planning a trip, starts with a thorough reading of the chart itself. There is a great deal of textual information on a nautical chart. The material may vary from chart to chart, but a typical one includes:

The chart's name and index number (this appears in several places); the scale at which the chart is drawn; date of the chart's publication (there are lists that can be consulted to see if you have the latest edition); the name of the agency publishing the chart; a scale showing nautical miles and possibly statute miles, feet, and yards; a scale by which fathoms, feet, and meters may be converted back and forth; various notes about pertinent regulations, warnings, and prohibitions; information about the unit (fathoms, feet, meters) in which soundings appear, and the level (mean low water?) on which they are based; ticks around the border, and often corresponding lines across the face of the chart, to show latitude and longitude; the index numbers of adjoining charts, arranged along the pertinent borders; several compass roses, showing both true and magnetic directions on outer and inner rings, respectively, along with the amount of magnetic variation, the year in which it was recorded, and the amount by which it may be expected to increase or decrease per year; a note listing the places, usually Coast Guard stations, where storm warnings are posted; an overprint and explanation of Loran lines, which are employed in electronic navigation; basic information about the range of tidal rise and fall at various points on the chart; a block of information about N.O.A.A. weather radio broadcasts in the vicinity; an 800 telephone number to call to report spills of oil or hazardous substances; and, quite possibly, the name of the ship whose survey provided data for the chart, along with the name of her commanding officer.

While a chart may be considered as timely as the month, date, and year printed on its lower left-hand corner, as soon as it is issued it starts becoming obsolete. New obstacles appear, buoys get shifted, church steeples get demolished to make way for shoe stores and burger franchises. The government issues publications, however, that advise sailors on changing conditions and often even provide corrected sections to be pasted over old charts. These documents are the weekly issues of *Notice to Mariners*, published by the Defense Mapping Agency's Hydrographic Center and prepared jointly with the National Ocean Survey and the Coast Guard. Individual Coast Guard districts also publish *Local Notices to Mariners*, which pay more attention to the sort of waters and conditions likely to be encountered by recreational sailors.

Charts also should be updated by something called *local knowledge*, which means exactly what it says: not the data collected by technologically sophisticated research ships and spy satellites, cartographers, commandants, and bureaucrats, but rather the information that is assembled by the people who actually use the water. It is these people, after all, who are the first to know when a channel silts up or changes its course, or when a red buoy "2" gets dragged under and obliterated by a barge that's shaving a turn. Local knowledge can be obtained from other recreational sailors or sport fishers, but it is most likely to come from people who make their livings on the water, the commercial fishers, for they are the people who must go out day after day, regardless of the weather.

Ideally, of course, you want a combination of local knowledge, well- and logically-placed aids to navigation, and a richly detailed chart. The trick is never to get into the position where you must make an important navigation decision on the basis of just one source of information. As the note found on most nautical charts says, "The prudent mariner will not rely solely on any single aid to navigation, particularly on floating aids."

You have read the chart. You know where you are, and you know where you want to go. The next step is to lay out your course.

I happen to be one of those map-lovers who cannot stand to have a map marked up. Back in prehistoric times when several members of the domestic petroleum cartel operated free public touring centers, I would drop in to get a map—say, of the eastern United States—and the person behind the counter would reach for the map with one hand, a thick-tipped marking pen poised for action in the other. "Where do you want to go?" he would ask me, and I had to be quick-witted enough to explain that I wanted the map *unmarked* before he was able to start marking it. Some were very fast on the draw, so to speak (it was, after all, their job), and occasionally I would lose; the map I took home with me was a disappointment—defiled, defaced, made somehow less than a map. It took me a while to learn that, regardless of my feelings about other maps, it is not only proper to place all sorts of marks on nautical charts; it is positively necessary to do so if you want them to serve their full purpose.

Because you'll be using your charts more than once, the marking is done with a fine-pointed *pencil*. A chunky *eraser* is also necessary, as are tools for drawing straight lines, measuring distances, and transferring compass angles from one part of the chart to the other. There are several commercial *plotting tools* on the market that do these jobs in interesting and ingenious ways, but the tools I use are a couple of plastic drafter's *triangles*, a plastic *protractor*, a set of *parallel rules*, and a pair of *dividers*. The triangles serve as straightedges and for a number of other odd jobs. The protractor is not absolutely necessary, but it is handy for checking your bearing and relative bearings to other objects.

The parallel rules are two plastic straightedges, maybe fourteen inches long, that are connected by moveable metal strips. The rules can be collapsed, like the pantograph of a trolley car, until they are side by side, or they can be opened so they are several inches apart or any distance in between, but they always remain parallel to each other. By placing one of them on the chart's printed compass rose at a desired angle (88° Magnetic, for instance), you can open the rules up and transfer the angle to another part of the chart. Or, after you have constructed the line on the chart that you want to represent your course, you can transfer the angle of that line to the rose and effortlessly read its compass angle off the rose. If your line and the rose are far apart, you can "walk" the rules from one to the other by successively opening and closing them.

Dividers are similar to the devices that were called compasses that you used in high school geometry to draw circles. (The pointed leg was the circle's center, and you twirled the leg with the pencil in it to create the circle.) In the case of dividers, though, both legs are pointed. They may be opened to various spans and used to measure distances on the chart and to transfer them to the mileage scale, and vice versa. They, too, may be "walked" for greater distances.

These few devices, along with the chart and the boat's compass, are really all the hardware you need to plan and follow your course.

You'll need a knowledge of the wind direction, because it will dictate to some extent the course you can take, and you may need to take current into consideration in a calculation about leeway, which will be touched on later. The chart will tell you about any obstacles in your way, and whether you'll have sufficient water depth to get where you're going. You may want to look around for a possible bailout point in case things don't turn out the way you want them to. Your course on the chart may or may not be a straight line. It will have to be a course you can really sail, not just a neat set of pencil marks on a pretty chart. It must represent your desires about where you'd like to go and how you'd like to get there, as influenced by actual conditions along the way. It must be subject to change as the conditions change. In addition to all this, you'll need as much local knowledge as you can gather. And common sense. And then the prudent mariner will be ready to go.

Suppose we've decided to sail from Oriental over to South River and to anchor out overnight. At some time before we want to leave, we assemble our information. This could be on the day before, or it could be during breakfast on the day we want to leave. It will not take long.

What do we know?

We know that South River is on the other side of the Neuse River (which is about three miles wide at Oriental) and downstream from where we are. Measured on a straight line, the entrance to South River is about five and a quarter miles away from where we'd put up our sails.

We know that on this particular day, the wind is from the west, which means it will be pretty well behind us for the duration of the sail. That means running and broad reaching on the way down, and, if the wind remains out of the west, as the weather radio informs us it probably will, beating our way back tomorrow. Experience leads us to expect that our average speed down will be about three and a half knots.

Now we choose our chart, or charts. According to *Nautical Chart Catalog 1*, which covers the Atlantic and Gulf Coasts, there are several possibilities. At least three charts cover both Oriental and the entrance to South River. But the scale on two of them—*Pamlico Sound, Western Part*, and *Portsmouth Island to Beaufort, Including Cape Lookout Shoals*— is 1:80,000, while the third has a scale of 1:40,000. This one, *Nautical Chart 11541, Intracoastal Waterway, Neuse River to Myrtle Grove Sound, North Carolina*, is a large-scale chart that's actually a collection of strip charts designed to assist the sailor who's using the Intracoastal Waterway, the protected and well-marked route that runs along much of the Eastern and Gulf coasts. One of its panels shows the area between Oriental and South River in excellent detail, just right for our short voyage. This particular series of charts

The course from Oriental to South River

comes in a handy folder that provides information on tides and on the services that are available at ports along the way.

The chart itself has all the data that are going to be so valuable to us—the warnings, prohibited areas, the aids to navigation, and a wealth of other information on what the water's like between our point of departure and our destination. Of truly overriding importance is what the chart has to say about water depths (which are reported here in feet, measured at m.l.w.), for the area we're sailing can be quite shallow, and it is necessary to use dredged channels if one is interested in exploring the wide creeks and rivers in a fixed-keel boat. It is just such opportunities for exploration that make the lower Neuse my favorite place in all the world to go sailing.

With the chart laid out in front of us on a flat surface (for example, the *chart table* in a cruising sailboat), we proceed to lay out our anticipated course in pencil.

There's only one logical way out of our marina berth in Whittaker Creek into the Neuse River, where we'll raise our sails, and that's the well-marked and -dredged channel, so we won't need to mark that portion of the course. But we will remember, when we leave the slip, that because we're going toward the sea, the red markers will be on our port side and the greens (or blacks) will be on the starboard. The chart shows our channel clearly: There's a series of aids to navigation, numbered (if you're headed outward) "7," "5," "4," and "2," with the last one in deep water in the river. After we leave Whittaker Creek by a green marker labeled "7," we will soon come to what the chart calls "Fl G 4sec 15ft '5'." If we were uncertain of what this meant, we could look it up in *Chart No. 1* and determine that it stood for a green light that flashes once every four seconds, that stands fifteen feet above the high water mark, and that has the number "5" marked on it.

Next we will come on the chart to a purple triangle with the slogan "R '4'" next to it. The triangle tips us off that this is an unlighted daybeacon, red in color, with a "4" on it. The chart encloses the 4 in quote marks in order to separate it from the profusion of other numbers nearby which refer to the water depth at mean low water. In the case of the water around "R '4'," the depth is about three feet. This furnishes us with great incentive to stay in the channel that "R '4'" helps define, since our boat draws four feet. We'll pass that even-numbered marker on our port side.

The next marker is not the "3" that might be expected. It is not unusual for one or more markers to be missing from numerical sequence. Remember, odd and even numbers are displayed on specific sides of the channel, and it may be that another green marker for the starboard side of the channel wasn't necessary at that point. So we come next to "Fl R 2.5sec 15ft '2'," another lighted marker that flashes at a set interval. Another clue that it is a light, and not a daybeacon, may be found in the little blip, a symbol sort of like a fat exclamation point or a skinny ascension balloon, that points to it. That is the symbol for a light, while the tiny triangle means a daybeacon.

After the "2," we'll be out of the channel and, according to the chart, in water that's more than six feet deep, and we no longer will be so dependent on lights and beacons to keep us from running aground. It is here that we'll be able to raise our sails and start off toward South River. So for planning purposes, that's where our trip will begin.

Because the wind will be from the west, we will be able to lay out our plot in straight lines, rather than a series of tacks. (To check on exactly where "west" is, we need only refer to the compass rose printed a half-foot away on our chart.) Laying a side of our triangle or one edge of the parallel rules on the chart, we sight a line from light number

"2" across and down the Neuse to the light that guards the entrance to our destination, the "Fl G 2.5sec 15ft 4M '1' PA." We're familiar with the Fl G and so on, but what's this "4M"? It's the first time we've encountered such a designation. *Chart No. 1* informs us that a capital "M" stands for "miles;" what "4M" means is that the light may be expected to be visible for that distance on a clear night. And "PA" means its position is approximate. Doubtless it must be moved from time to time to safely mark the entrance of a river that is constantly scouring new channels and depositing new loads of sediment. So we should not be unduly alarmed if, when we arrive at "1," we find it slightly askew from its charted position.

Our straight line across and down the river takes us quite close to an area of shallower water, known as Garbacon Shoal. (The chart provides a finely dotted line and a bluish tint for water shallower than six feet, which is a helpful visual aid for skippers, regardless of their boats' draft. It really is amazing how much useful information is packed into a nautical chart.) On this occasion, at least, we want to be super-cautious about getting into too-shallow water. (The chart shows the six-foot line very clearly, but how are we to know, once we're under sail, exactly where it is? In real life, the Neuse River does not come with dotted lines and bluish tints. Our boat is equipped with a depth finder, but we learned long ago that depth finders rarely work when you want them to.) So our super-caution leads us to break the course into two pieces.

The logical dividing point is the daybeacon that sticks out of the water about half way between Oriental and South River—the triangle labeled "W 'B' PA Priv maintd," meaning white, lettered "B," privately maintained, position approximate. If we go to the north of "B," we surely will avoid the shallow water. The result is two pencil lines on the chart, one from the "2" down near Oriental to just north of the "B," and the other from near the "B" to the "1" at South River.

Using the parallel rules, we compare the angle of the first course segment to the "magnetic" section of the compass rose. It is approximately 112° Magnetic, a course toward the southeast. With the pencil, we write "C 112 M" above the line. The "C" stands for "course," and there is no need to add the symbol for "degrees." Now, when the boat is under way, we know that by keeping its heading at 112° by the boat's compass, and by compensating for any sideways push we may be getting from the current, we may reasonably expect to end up just to the port side of the white daybeacon named "B."

Now for the second leg, from "B" to "1." Our course line here translates into 132° Magnetic, or almost directly toward the southeast.

Our course is now pretty much set. If we can steer the boat along the headings of 112° and then 132°, we should have no difficulty getting where we want to go. But it is nice, too, to know how long our trip will take and to anticipate what we'll be seeing along the way and when we'll be seeing it. We can get that sort of information by engaging in a few more calculations involving speed and distance.

Using the dividers or a ruler, we check the distance from our departure point to our turning point and from there to our destination. By transferring this distance to the mileage scale, we learn that it will be about three nautical miles from "2" at Oriental to the "B" in mid-river, and about two and a quarter miles from "B" to "1." We enter the distances and speeds beneath the course lines, "D 3" and "D 2.25" and "S 3.5." So the total trip, excluding motoring out from the slip at one end and motoring in to our anchorage at the other, will be something more than five miles—let's say five and a half, to be on the safe side.

We've estimated that our average speed under sail will

be three and a half knots in a wind of the sort we'll have today. Reaching deep back into grade school mathematics, we recall that

$$\text{TIME} = \frac{\text{DISTANCE}}{\text{SPEED}}$$

and that brings us to a sailing time of a little more than one and one-half hours. This is only an approximation, but it is a very helpful one. We know now that if we leave by mid-morning, there'll be abundant time for the sail and plenty of daylight for getting through the channel at the other end, anchoring, and exploring in the dinghy before starting dinner. A glance at the tide tables shows that there'll be plenty of water in the channel at the time we want to go through it. We know that shouldn't be a problem anyway, since the chart shows channel depths of twenty-one, thirteen, and ten feet over there, but we've been consulting some fonts of local knowledge and have learned that there are some bumps on the bottom that the National Oceanic and Atmospheric Administration isn't aware of but that the local shrimp fleet knows intimately.

While we're at it, we might as well consult our chart for what we're going to see along the way. Using the triangles and dividers and distance scale, we see that about one and a half nautical miles after we get the sails up, or a little under half an hour after our departure, we should find ourselves abreast of two aids to navigation. On our starboard, less than half a mile away and thus easily identifiable, will be the flashing light named "7" that guards Garbacon Shoal and that serves as a turning point for traffic on the Intracoastal Waterway. The legend "Ra Ref" means that it contains a radar reflector. Almost simultaneously, we should sight to our port, about three-quarters of a mile away, a privately maintained white marker labeled "A."

When our boat is precisely on a line connecting the two, we are *on a range*. You will recall that *ranges* are aids to navigation that are deliberately set up to show a sailor when he is in the right place and when he isn't. But a lot of information about position can be obtained by checking on *any* two identifiable objects. When they and the boat all line up on the water, a line can be drawn through them on the chart and the boat can be assumed to be somewhere on that line, which is called a *line of position*, or *LOP* for short. In this case, we'd also be on another line of position—the almost perpendicular one created by our course line. Where the two lines intersect is a *fix*. Fixes are positions that are accurately established, and they are very important in navigation. If our fix from the two LOPs is correct, we should be somewhere near the twenty-four-foot depth mark on the chart. "Somewhere near" is about as close as we'd want to assume, since we may have strayed off our original course line and since we know that one of the aids that make up our range, the white "A," has a position that is approximate.

About a mile and a half farther on, we should be rounding the white daybeacon lettered "B" and moving into the second leg of our course. If we note the time it took us to get this far, we will be able to calculate our actual average speed (speed is distance divided by time) and file it away for future reference. If it differs markedly from our original estimate of three and a half knots, we may want to recalculate our estimated arrival time.

With the boat on the new course of 132°, we'll find the wind coming more from our beam and we will need to adjust the sails. As we travel the remaining two and a quarter miles toward South River, we'll be drawing gradually closer to the land on the other side of the Neuse. There'll be plenty of time to marvel at the fact that a great deal of it looks, from the water at least, unspoiled. We will be reluctant to drop the sails when we reach the flashing green "1," for that will mean cranking up the smelly, noisy little engine, but we hesitate to pass into the somewhat narrow and curving channel under wind power alone.

It is a marked channel, not terribly unlike the one we left behind at Oriental, but the chart shows some differences, which we should review while planning the trip. For one thing, we are going from larger waters into smaller, so now it's *red right returning*. For another, we see that the sequence of markers goes from green "1" to red "2" to a green marker labeled "WR 3." Beside the label is a symbol that looks something like a comic-strip rendition of a fish skeleton after a cat has finished with it. *Chart No. 1* informs us that this means we'll be approaching (and passing on our port, since the marker is black) a beacon guarding a sunken wreck that is "dangerous to surface navigation" because it is in less than eleven fathoms of water.

The next marker is shown on the chart to be a green daybeacon numbered "5." And this is a surprise to us, because our previous edition of this chart showed the marker—erroneously—to be numbered "3." The reason we know it was incorrect was our own local knowledge: We observed the beacon on our last visit to South River, saw it was really a "5," and marked the change on the chart at the time, in ink. Charts, like everything else, are imperfect. And nautical charts, more than any other kind of maps, are *living* documents. It may well be that when we pass the sunken wreck today, the daybeacon will have been changed again. But at least we know enough from experience not to be panicked if it turns out to be something that's not on the chart.

Now that we're through the channel into South River, we could explore for several miles. Our copy of the *Coast Pilot* states that the main channel of the river "had reported depths of eight feet for about six miles above the entrance, thence seven feet for another one and one-half miles" when it was surveyed several years before. A friend back in Oriental told us about an artesian spring that bubbles out under the water a mile or so up the river. But on this voyage we decide to anchor a short distance in, off the abandoned village of Lukens. Many years ago, the fishing families who populated Lukens were driven away by hurricanes. Most loaded their possessions and even homes onto barges and moved to Oriental, and little remains of the town now except for a few pieces of foundation, some paths, a well-tended graveyard, and a contraption that looks suspiciously as if it had been employed in the manufacture of distilled spirits.

We will drop the hook, get our lights and lanterns ready for the night, check the weather radio, erase all of today's pencil lines, congratulate ourselves on having navigated them so well, and row the dinghy in to Lukens. We will keep a sharp eye open once we're on land; local knowledge speaks of 400-pound black bears that have not yet been told they live in an industrialized, technological society and therefore must be almost extinct. There will be plenty of time to explore, to rest, and to make the plans for tomorrow's travels.

3

THE OTHER
SAILING

CHAPTER EIGHT

Experience

And there are the nuts and bolts that are learned in the best way of all: through experience.

Perhaps when one is very young, one's physical and mental muscles are in such good tone that two or three passes at something new are sufficient to imprint that something on the learner's mind. A whole world of experience and wonder is out there, and the inquisitive young person knows that there lies ahead a lifetime of feelings, colors, shapes, smells, tastes, and events, and so she gulps down whole headsful of experience, loading the millions of cells of her memory with it, reveling in the exquisite satisfactions of recalling it and matching it and combining it with other new experiences, filing it away and then drawing it out when it is needed again. The memory cells seem unlimited in number and in their ability and trustworthiness and suppleness.

But the aging process is, among other things, a deteriorating process, and the memory and the ability to manage one's memory do not always function the way one wants them to. With each cigarette that is smoked, in those years before good sense and fear of death finally win out and the coffin tacks are at last set aside for good, the body and the brain are damaged a little more. With every swig of booze, each glass of wine, the memory chokes a bit. But at the same time, the experiences, and the material generated by them that requires remembering, show no signs of abating. They pile up. By the time it is middle aged, the brain may have so many demands on it that it may occasionally refuse. It is as if the memory decides to put its foot down; to declare:

"How do I know that this thing you want me to remember is really worth remembering? What about all that junk you made me learn before? Remember when we lived in Atlanta? Of course you remember. Remember all those streets and politicians' names you made me remember? What good do they do you now? None at all! You lived in Atlanta for three years, and yet every time you go back you manage to get lost. You blame it on the one-way streets and new buildings, but you and I know better. And how many of the politicians do you remember? Maybe one. And that's because he got elected president. And you're well on your way to forgetting *him* now. I just don't trust you any more when you tell me something's of 'lasting importance'. You said that last year about the area code for Los Angeles, and I bet you haven't called L.A. twice since then."

And so the memory refuses to learn more, or at least it refuses to learn more *easily*. No longer can you casually toss it a fact or a snippet of experience and expect it to file the item away in the proper folder and to produce it instantly on demand. By the time of your middle years, you may find that you have to force your memory to absorb and retain your experiences; you have to insist that it believe (and sometimes even trick it into believing) that a given experience is truly important to you, that it is not just more of the same junk mail, the same undialed area codes.

There grows out of all this, fortunately, a tradeoff. It may be more difficult in middle age to learn something and to keep it learned, but when it *is* learned, when it *does* make it through all those obstacles that your stubbornly disobedient memory has set up, it turns out to mean more. It is more valuable, and it stays learned. Quantity may be down, but quality is 'way up. In order to get through the obstacles, a prospective bit of new material for the memory has had to survive an ordeal of skepticism, doubting, and testing that all the rest of your memory and experience have thrown in its way.

Back when you were a youth, your unquestioning brain accepted experiences at their face value and filed them away uncritically. But now everything you ask the brain to remember must prove its worthiness. If it isn't top-notch and really important to you, it will be discarded in a particularly devious way: Your brain will assure you that it's been filed, but at some convenient moment, when you aren't looking, the brain will quietly and effortlessly dump the thought into the trash can marked "forgotten." All in all, it's a fairly efficient process, but it can be quite maddening at times.

One day toward the end of the stay at Walloon, Strat and I were out on the lake in the Ensign. The sailing and the learning had been going very well. We were well past the classroom stage. I looked upon our excursions as small voyages in which something was always being learned, and in which lessons that had been learned before were reinforced and broadened by repetition and trial and error, but also as outings in which the learning was not at the expense of having a good time. It was both fun and education: Strat and I would go sailing down the lake and back—and along the way, *all* along the way, there was learning to be had.

I learned, in this manner, how to move away from the mooring and how to approach it at the end of the sail. (I wrote before that you time your shoot in to the mooring so that when the boat stops "you reach over the side and shackle a line from the bow to an eye in the float." But how do you know when to start the approach so that the boat stops at the right place? The answer is that you get out on the water and try it, over and over again, until you find a sequence that works.) I learned how to coil the loose ends of my halyards when we were sailing, so they didn't get in the way and cause confusion, but could be gotten to and used quickly in the event a sail had to be lowered. I asked Strat if he knew the name of the coiling routine, and he said he didn't. "We can just call it 'Strat's knot'," he said.

I learned that one of the premier tradeoffs of sailing in Petoskey occurred when the wind was out of the west, as it often is at Walloon, and we would sail easily down the lake, our canvas out wing-and-wing style, making good time, chatting away, moving in a fairly straight line toward the narrow channel that separates two of Walloon's arms; and then, after agreeing that it was about time to head back, finding that it would take a dozen or more tacks, and a great deal more time, to return to the mooring. And I started learning how to get the most out of my tacks. Because of the hills and trees bordering Walloon, the shore of the lake could receive very little wind at the same time the center was getting a lot. So sometimes it would be wiser to sail a series of shorter tacks in the center section of the lake rather than to stretch them out so they almost kissed the shores.

Strat had the tiller as we went through the narrows, which is marked by two privately maintained stakes, and I took us through on the return. And once when I had the tiller we approached a profusion of sailboats from a summer camp, each of them going in its own particular direction, and I gratefully handed the helm to Strat and watched how he expertly negotiated our heavier boat through the traffic.

But I knew all that time that something very important was missing from my education. I still had no sense of where the wind was. I still could be surprised by the fact that, with my hand firmly on the tiller, we could unexpectedly turn so far toward the wind that we would be in irons; or that, while sailing downwind on what I thought was a proper broad reach, we would suddenly start to jibe. I simply could not feel the wind; I did not know where it was coming from. Or I would feel it and then lose it. Adding to this complication, which is an extremely serious one for anybody who wants to be a sailor, was the fact that when wind-confusion set in, it invariably brought on tiller-confusion. I would see, or feel, that I had steered the boat around so the wind was no longer coming from where it should (which is the self-centered sailor's way of saying that we were no longer pointed where we should have been pointed) and then, in an attempt to remedy this, I would speculatively push or pull on the tiller, and about fifty percent of the time I would be wrong. The boat would go still farther in the wrong direction, the sails would react even more angrily to this insult, and Strat would say something very diplomatically about how it might be better if we did such-and-such. The strains on him must have been enormous, especially on those occasions when the condition I was leading us into was a potentially head-splitting jibe. But Strat was a gentleman, and he was patient, and he also may have been remembering the time when he was becoming a sailor.

It seemed almost as if I were destined not to learn about the wind. I wondered if that were the case, and I wondered whether it was possible for someone who lacked that aptitude to enjoy sailing, or whether that was an automatic disqualification—something on the order of a monotone's being an unlikely candidate for the Metropolitan Opera. I asked Strat, and Strat said, "Oh, I wouldn't worry about it. One day it'll just happen."

One day it did just happen. It was toward the end of the stay in Michigan. The weather had been grim for the previous couple of days, with wave after wave of low, rainy clouds sweeping in from Lake Michigan like the breakers on an ocean beach in a storm. Occasionally the clouds would thin and the ceiling would lift and I would look out at the Ensign anchored in the lake, but then another battalion of grey clouds would double-time across from the west. This is often the pattern in the upper part of lower Michigan. It is one of the reasons the place is so attractively verdant. But at the moment I had difficulty appreciating that; my time on the farm was running out, and there was so much more sailing I wanted to do.

Then, that August morning, the sun rose across the lake and did not follow its recent pattern of disappearing for the rest of the day into a bank of low clouds. Patches, then acres of blue appeared in the sky. By mid-morning it was a fine day, with a moderate breeze and a touch of crispness that reminded me that autumn comes early up here.

Strat was at work and couldn't sail. I gathered some cheese and pita bread, a hard-cooked egg, and a couple of soft drinks, and rowed out to the Ensign. Within a few minutes I was headed down the lake, the mainsail well out. After about a mile I hardened up toward the wind so I had made an almost complete reversal of my course. A large cloud, which had been approaching from the west, obscured the sun and it suddenly felt ten degrees cooler. The wind dropped and the lake's surface became mirror-like. It was quiet; there were no water skiiers out that day. I was in no particular hurry, so I leaned back in the cockpit, the main sheet loose in my hand, the same hand resting gently on the tiller. I ate a bite of cheese and contemplated the world.

Then, far away down the lake, I saw a million pinpoints appear on the surface, as if a tremendous number of goldfish had decided to graze all at the same time. The pinpoints covered an elliptical section of the lake, and the entire oval was moving across the water toward me. I knew, because Strat and I had talked about it before, that this was an effect of the wind on the water called a cat's-paw. It was caused by the landforms on the shore that sheltered some parts of the lake more than others: a portion of the surface that was protected from the wind by a hill would be calm and flat and almost oily-shiny; right next to it would be a section covered with pinpoints. When we would sail out of the shiny water into the other, the sails would immediately fill with new wind.

This time I was almost becalmed, and the wind was moving toward me with a clarity I had never seen before. I watched it curve swiftly, smoothly toward the boat, almost as one observes events with detachment in a dream. I could see the wind's very direction. I pushed the tiller away, hoping I had enough steerageway to move the boat to a more favorable angle with the wind when it arrived. All of this happened quietly, almost so quietly as to be eerie. I realized that I was no longer detached, but now was holding my breath as I watched the curtain cross the water.

At the moment it touched the sails, it touched my face. I clearly felt the wind on my cheek, as soft as a feather but as tangible as anything I had ever experienced. I turned my head to the side; the feeling disappeared from my cheek and touched the back of my neck. I turned my head back, and the feather moved around to my cheek again. The sails filled and the boat picked up speed. I could hear the sound of water moving past the stern. My face still told me where the wind was coming from. All the way back to the mooring I tested the new sensation, turning my head first this way and then that, trying to trick my cheeks and neck, in the way that you test new eyeglasses. My face passed the test. I had become able to tell where the wind was coming from. And, having learned it, I have kept it. It has become part of my basic inventory, along with qualities like balance and depth perception. A week later I was home in New York, waiting in a grubby subway station for an even grubbier subway train, and I felt the faintest trace of moving air on my right cheek. I leaned out from the platform and peered down the tracks. There, at least ten blocks away, were the headlights of the train. It was moving toward me, pushing through the tunnel a long column of air that I had never been able to feel before.

△ △ △

By this time I had become thoroughly devoted to sailing, and the foul breath of the subway only made me itch all the more for the real air, the kind that can be found in sails. That is not so easily found in the town where I live. New York City, despite its location on several bodies of water (an ocean, a bay, two major rivers, several lesser streams, and a sound), is not a sailing town. It is difficult to get close to the water in New York, and when you do get close to it you often find it is very unattractive.

In desperation one fine spring weekend, I went through the Yellow Pages. There was someone in Far Rockaway who rented sailboats. Far Rockaway is a thin peninsula, a sort of Atlantic barrier beach carried to its inevitable, densely overpopulated, heavily abused conclusion, that hangs down below New York City maybe nine miles from

Times Square. It is part of the city's Queens borough. On its front side is the Atlantic Ocean. On the back is Jamaica Bay, an area of perhaps fifteen square miles, of which almost half is grassy marsh that floods at high tide and that the builders and politicians haven't yet found a convenient way to destroy. (Some of it, in fact, now is included in Gateway National Park, a relatively natural area that covers portions of the urban wetlands of both New York and New Jersey.)

My wife and I found the rental place with some difficulty, the street-naming and -numbering system being rather casual in Far Rockaway. It was on a channel on the bay side, and it actually was a commercial boat yard whose owner had a couple of Lasers for rent. The Laser is a board boat, fourteen feet long and similar in configuration to the Sunfish. It is rigged as a catboat, with one sail.

The owner of the boat yard asked about my experience. I'd sailed a Pearson Ensign for two weeks the previous summer, I told him. I was a novice, but a serious novice. That seemed good enough for him. We walked down to the floating dock, he showed us how to mount the mast and sail, we climbed aboard, and off we went. We sailed down the short channel into the bay.

The breeze was brisk and the sun was out brightly, warming us and the water and making it a splendid day. We sailed close to the wind, toward the west, for a while. On our starboard were the runways of John F. Kennedy International Airport, and in the distance to the northwest were the tops of the twin World Trade Center towers, the uninspiring boxes that have overwhelmed the majestic Empire State Building as Manhattan's most noticeable landmarks. The excitement of sailing was made all the more delicious by the knowledge that we were doing it right on the front porch of a city quite intolerant of the environment and of such purportedly outmoded technologies as sail power.

A Forgiving Wind

We fell off gradually and started downwind. The Laser was exceptionally fast-moving, compared to the Ensign, or perhaps it only seemed that way because we were sitting so much closer to the water. The wind picked up—or, again, perhaps it only seemed that way. It seemed to be filling the sail and then some. I loosened the sheet some more, as I would on the larger boat, to allow a bit of the wind to spill from the sail. Soon the sail was flying perpendicular to the boat. On the Ensign it would have been resting against the shrouds, but the Laser had no shrouds. Then it got a little forward of perpendicular. That's when we went over.

We both fell into the water, but I held onto the main sheet so we stayed with the boat. We righted it (we'd read up on this in advance, since it happens so frequently; you simply use the daggerboard as a lever to flip the boat upright) and my wife climbed aboard. She held the boat steady while I started aboard myself. Then the sheet became jammed on a piece of hardware. The sail filled with wind, too much wind, and the boat went partly over again. I fell off and the boat sailed away.

I dogpaddled a few seconds, then decided to test my life preserver, which I wear fairly religiously because I'm not the world's best swimmer, and found that it did what it was supposed to do. Then I discovered that my feet were touching a muddy, oozing bottom. I tried not to think of what was lodged down there in the muck or even in the moving waters of Jamaica Bay, which has served New York City as a convenient sewer for a very long time.

My wife got the sheet untangled and sailed the boat around and I finally got aboard. We checked for damage, found none, and started downwind again. We joked about how the main danger in dumping ourselves in Jamaica Bay was not drowning, but hepatitis. A 747 owned by Delta screamed into the sky a few hundred feet above our heads and I wondered if we had provided a planeload of Atlanta-bound passengers with some diversion. An aerial dock committee, I thought. Then we went over again.

We finally made it back by way of a series of very careful downwind tacks, and the operator of the boat yard was on the dock to meet us. Our landing, thank goodness, was without incident.

"We went over a couple of times," I said.

"Yeah, I know," he said. "I saw you up the channel there."

"But we had a fine time," I said.

"Good," he replied. "It's a great day for a sail."

"I'm still not exactly sure what happened," I said.

"You let the sail get ahead of the mast when you were going downwind," he said. "On a one-sail boat that can be trouble. There's no jib, like you were used to on the Ensign, to balance out the push on the main. The wind just takes the main on out until it gets ahead of the mast and then it keeps going, and something has to give, and what usually gives is the boat. It turns right over. You don't have that heavy keel down there to hold you up."

I told him that was surely what had happened, and that I was grateful for his explanation.

"There's no substitute for experience," he said.

△ △ △

In the soft, pastel light of dawn the sailboat looked about twice as big as it had the night before, when I had arrived in Oriental and walked down to the dock to take a look at it. And even then I had been convinced that *Arena* was far too large for me ever to learn to sail.

It was now the fall of the year in which I fell in love with sailing. There had been the original visit to Sailcraft, and then the weeks sailing the Ensign in Michigan. Now I had been drawn back to Oriental. The itching for sailing had continued, and I had called Andy Denmark and asked his advice on renting boats. The correct word is "chartering," he said; he knew someone who docked his boat at Sailcraft who might be interested in chartering it to us. It was Blaine Liner, the fellow who had re-introduced me to Andy in the first place.

I had protested in a half-hearted way, tempered by my excitement over the prospect. We didn't know enough about sailing to take a cruising sailboat out into fairly open water. Liner's boat was larger than anything I'd ever been on, much less sailed, unless you count the night I slept on *Odyssey*. I would be terrified of damaging it. And so on. I had about a dozen solid reasons. Hogwash, replied Andy. He is the sort of person who believes in learning to swim by jumping into the water, or learning to fly by simply grabbing the controls of an airplane. I am sure his system works well for him, but I usually require a good deal more preparation and testing. He was confident that I could do it, and what I didn't know I would pick up quickly. I still protested. Andy offered a compromise.

We could charter Liner's boat for a week. We'd take it day-sailing for a couple of days and get the feeling of it, and then Andy and Mary would take *Odyssey* out and we would cruise, in both boats, down and across the river to anchorages Andy knew. My terrors persisted, but I agreed. As it worked out, we scheduled the cruise for the week of Thanksgiving. That would be taking some risk with the weather—it could very well be chilly and rainy the whole time—but the chances were it would be a fine set of eastern North Carolina fall days, with cool nights and warm, sunny days and bright blue skies. "Plus the fact that by then the mosquitoes'll be down to the size of sparrows," said Andy.

So it was arranged. Liner seemed happy to charter his boat to us, even after I explained very carefully my considerable lack of experience (I wondered what incredible exaggerations Andy had laid on him). I had a southern trip coming up anyway, and my wife had business a couple hundred miles away, so we agreed that I would drive down and get checked out in the operation of the boat and she would fly in at the beginning of the charter week. We'd have plenty of time to get accustomed to the boat—not only to sailing it, but also to living on it—before we took it out overnight.

Arena was a twenty-seven-foot-long boat made by Hunter, on the smallish side as cruising boats go, but I knew nothing of relative size back then. Now, in the dawn, I stood on the solid, grey-timbered dock waiting for Blaine to arrive, and I tried to figure things out. There seemed to be about twice as many wires and lines running from the deck up to the mast as I could determine uses for. The boat was vastly more complex-looking than the Ensign. I had no idea where the jib sheets should go after they left the sail's clew. (I hadn't a clew.) The shiny, powerful-looking winches back on both sides of the cockpit gave me some ideas, but I couldn't for the life of me decide where the blocks, the pulleys which route the sheets around the cabin and standing rigging, should be placed.

The boat was docked in its own berth, in a slip between two short finger piers that extended at right angles from the main dock out into Whittaker Creek. I could see the current flowing along the stream, which was about twenty yards wide at that point, through the wider cove and then toward the great mouth of the river, and I knew that beyond that was the sound and, eventually, the ocean.

It was later, much later, that I developed the ability to register automatically, in that portion of my brain that I had so recently and brashly decided to reserve for matters of nautical importance, information on the strength of that current and its direction—bits of information that are of great value to a sailor in tidal waters. Now, several years later, my memory has no difficulty in recalling, even though they seemed of no importance to me at the time and did not even enter my consciousness, two things that any sailor should have known that morning and should have filed away even if they did not seem immediately useful: that the tide was going out and that it was ebbing at the rate of about half a knot. A half-knot is not intense enough to cause much trouble, but it must be taken into account. (Much of the trouble that *is* caused in sailing wouldn't be trouble if it were anticipated.)

I paid, back then, absolutely no mind to a number of other fragments of information that were every bit as important as the drift and set of the current. The condition of the sky was one. Another was the direction of the wind. I had glanced at the sky as any landlubber would, more in awe of the sunrise than anything else, and in thankfulness for its clear autumn blueness. But I had not known to read it for the detail and portent that an experienced sailor seeks.

As for the wind, I knew that there was virtually none, as often is the case at dawn, but I did not know to find the one or two tufts of high clouds that moved placidly toward the northeast and that promised a good, unsurprising day of sailing. I thought nothing of these things, because all my energies of judgment were devoted to wondering how a twenty-seven-foot sailing boat, even with the assistance of a powerful little diesel engine, could possibly move backwards out into that tidal stream and swing its bow around for the trip out into the channel and into open water. The angles all seemed too sharp, Whittaker Creek far too narrow. And, now that I noticed it, the current seemed a little too fast. With the Ensign, current had not been a factor.

And the Ensign had its home at a mooring, surrounded by acres of water. Here the slip was only a couple of feet wider than the boat itself; cracking into it, either departing or returning, could cause a lot of trouble. I realized, totally and profoundly in a rush that almost took my breath away, how overwhelmingly ignorant I was of the whole thing, and I realized that twenty-four hours from then, after that day's shakedown cruise with the owner, I would be responsible for *Arena* for a week.

That night my wife would arrive in Oriental and we would start living aboard. I, so intensely aware now of my ignorance and inadequacy, would be her skipper. I thought very seriously about backing out then and there. Maybe nobody would laugh at us too much if we just lived on *Arena* at the dock for a week—used the boat as a pleasant base of operations while we explored the countryside. (I had already noticed that along Sailcraft's dock and the docks of other marinas in Oriental there were several boats that seemed never to go out, even though their owners came on weekends and lived on them and invited others down.) Or maybe the weather would turn miserable, and I could sit around at the dock and gripe about how my week of sailing had been cruelly snatched from me. I was coming up with some pretty awful scenarios when *Arena*'s owner arrived and said, "Let's go." I went, and decided to keep my fears to myself for a while—at least until I saw what sailing on *Arena* was like.

"Remember, *red right returning*," said Blaine as we motored out the channel from the cove into the river. *Arena*'s sails were down and Blaine stood flatfooted in the cockpit with one hand on the tiller and the other resting lightly on the motionless boom. He looked happy, free of serious worries. He seemed totally different from the man I had seen half a year ago back in his busy office. He had looked then, like many of us, tired and frazzled by the workload he had imposed on himself. Here he had shed his three-piece business suit for faded blue jeans, tattered deck shoes, a little cap, and a wool sweater that was obviously much loved. His face seemed to have lost its indoor paleness and to have become healthier, ruddier. He looked as if he cared about only one thing in the world: sailing *Arena*. It was a condition I would see, as time passed, in other sailors too, and before long I would see it in myself.

I sat in the cockpit forward of Blaine, my arm comfortably draped along the gunwale. It was a beautiful day. From here, *Arena* didn't look so enormous, and her size hadn't troubled us at all in leaving the slip. The throbbing of the diesel was disconcerting, but I knew it would soon end.

The square green daymarkers, some bearing lights, passed on our right as we eased out of the channel. Great grey seabirds, looking full of wisdom, perched on each of the posts that the Coast Guard had thoughtfully planted in the water, the pilings that bore the aids to navigation required by us humans. Each bird watched us as we went by—observed us without fear or comment, without even much curiosity. We were, for them, just part of the life of the water. The reddish-orange markers, which I knew would have to be on our right when we returned to our anchorage, were now on our left. Blaine steered a solid course among the markers and beacons, unhesitating but still cautious. He frequently looked back to make sure we were traveling a straight line. If you only watched the markers in front of you, he said, it was easy to stray out of the channel and run aground.

"How wide is the channel?" I asked. I had the chart for the lower Neuse in my hand but it paid only a minimal degree of attention to the channel or to the cove from which we'd just emerged. On it, we were traveling between two closely parallel dashed lines.

"Ten feet wide," said Blaine. His face was absolutely deadpan.

"*Ten feet?*" The boat itself was more than nine feet wide.

"In your mind it should be ten feet," he said. "Then you'll never run aground coming out of the channel."

We left the last channel marker, the Fl R 2.5sec 15ft "2," on our left, and I could tell from the strong, firm motion of the waves that we were in deeper water now. The chart said eight feet at mean low tide, which is fairly deep for the North Carolina sounds. Out in the middle of the river it would be around twenty feet.

The wind was different out in the river, which at this point was relatively open. It came from the same direction as before, but it was stronger, more certain of its identity than it had been during our protected run out the channel. For me, with all my other concerns that day, it was a little frightening. Frightening but also exhilarating. I have since then experienced that combination of feelings frequently while on the water, and I know it now as one of the more pleasing aspects of sailing.

Blaine took us well past the last beacon and headed *Arena*'s bow into the wind. He left the engine running but slipped the gear into neutral. "Time to go sailing," he said, and he started loosening the shock cords that held the mainsail wrapped snugly against the boom. I went forward to hank on the jib. I was pretty confident that I could do that particular task correctly; I'd spent an extraordinary amount of time the day before practicing mentally everything I knew about sailing, and hanking on a jib is pretty much the same from one boat to another.

The mystery of where the blocks for the jib sheets should go was quickly solved (they snapped through any of the dozens of holes in the metal railings that ran along the gunwales; this feature makes the tension on the jib almost infinitely adjustable), and the sails were up. Blaine gathered the free ends of the halyards into neat coils, the same ones that Strat had showed me. I asked him for the name of the coil, and he said he just called it "Liner's knot." He killed the engine and tossed the ignition key into the galley sink, just inside the cabin. Immediately *Arena* stopped bobbing in the waves. She started to feel like a sailboat. There was a beautiful quiet all around us.

It wasn't *really* quiet, for the wind and the slap of the waves and various of the boat's own sounds that I couldn't decipher yet—these all added up to a lot more than utter silence. But they were *natural* sounds, where before the overwhelming sensation had been the pounding of the small but insistent diesel.

We sailed for four hours that day, with Blaine explaining it all very thoughtfully and very well and with me taking notes in a notebook that I still have. The tacks and runs were long and fast in comparison with those I had had on Walloon, for we had much more water to play with. With the wind on our side we sailed over to the "7" light that marked Garbacon Shoal, then with it almost directly behind us and with the boom way out we headed east and I searched in vain for a daymarker that appeared on the chart but not in the real world. I learned that day what I had long ago learned about backpacking: Maps are fine; perhaps even wonderful; but they're also imperfect.

Blaine handed me the tiller, and I took it eagerly. He explained what a "forgiving" boat *Arena* was, by which he meant you could make a lot of mistakes with her and she'd let you get away with them. He demonstrated how it was possible to drop the tiller and go down into the cabin for a moment without any serious repercussions. That was a new and pleasant experience for me, since with the Ensign it wasn't wise to leave the helm at all (and it was almost impossible for me to get into the tiny cabin). And the winds here were steady, in strength and in direction, so we sailed with the sheets that controlled both main and jib fastened down to cleats that could be quickly released. On Walloon, with its constantly changing winds, it was unwise to fasten the sheets down. You had to be ready to give them slack if a puff came along. *Arena* was a much larger and heavier boat than the Ensign, and the things that happened, when they happened, seemed to happen in a much more controllable fashion.

"I think you'll do fine and have a great time," said Blaine after I'd sailed *Arena* for an hour or so. "How do you feel about it?"

"I was terrified when we started," I said. "I almost backed out. It's amazing, but I don't feel that way now. I know there's a lot I've got to learn, but I'm not paralyzed with fear the way I was before. Maybe I shouldn't be saying this, but I feel almost confident.'

"Sounds normal to me," said Blaine. "You and your wife're going to have a fine cruise. You want to head back?"

I said I did, and brought *Arena's* bow around a bit into a more close-hauled course and headed toward the marker at Garbacon Shoal. I knew that from there we could easily see the landmarks that would allow us to find the channel to Whittaker Creek and the marina. I felt fine. The boat seemed a lot easier to understand than I had expected, and much of what I had known about sailing came back to me with ease, even though three months had passed since I'd really been out on the water.

I hadn't committed any grievous errors. I was looking forward to my wife's arrival that night, to the trip to the village grocery store tomorrow for provisioning, and then to the beginning of our first sailboat cruise. Blaine leaned back in the cockpit, the comfortable, orange autumn sun on his face. He opened a can of beer, took a sip, put it down, idly picked up a life preserver—it had once been a brilliant international orange but now was faded by sunlight and salt air—and tossed it into the water.

"Man overboard," he said, calmly, deliberately. It took me two or three moments to understand what was happening. This was a rescue drill.

"*Woman* overboard. Pretend it's your wife." The life vest was drifting away behind us. It was getting smaller rapidly. If it had been a person, that person soon would be out of sight. Blaine was looking at his wristwatch.

"The water's sixty-eight degrees," he said. "That's not terribly comfortable." I pulled the tiller toward me, pushed it away, pulled it in again crazily, then realized that I'd better decide what I wanted to do and do it. I pulled the tiller firmly toward me and eased the main sheet. *Arena*, which had been sailing close to the wind on a port tack, began taking the wind more from the beam, then the stern as we curved around to starboard.

I had no idea of what my plan would result in, and after the maneuver started I even lost track of the direction of the wind. There was no section of my face that detected the breeze better than any other. I felt it all over my face. I felt my face flushing, with excitement and embarrassment and the early stages of panic. And I didn't have any real idea of where we were on the water. All through the sail I had kept an eye on the horizons, watching the shapes of the land and placing us and *Arena* in their framework. I knew where to look to find the bridge that was the first sign of Oriental, and I knew where to find the last daymarker or light we had passed. But now nothing seemed to fall into place.

"Forty seconds," said Blaine. "She's getting kind of cold."

At about the same time I realized that we were headed for a jibe, we jibed. The boom swung violently from the starboard to the port side, the sails filled with two loud *whumps*, and the boat heeled suddenly and steeply. I was obviously straining *Arena*'s forgiving nature, not to mention her mast and rigging. I remembered then what I had learned, or thought I had learned, about jibes. In a controlled jibe, you haul in the main sheet tightly, then ration it out carefully as the wind pushes the boom to the other side. It's the uncontrolled, unanticipated jibes that cause trouble, the cracked heads and mast. Neither of these happened this time. Blaine, who had seen the jibe coming even though I hadn't, kept his head well down, and the luck that protects idiots kept my skull from being halved. "Seventy seconds," said Blaine. "She's getting cold and *angry*. And you just jibed. Know where the wind's coming from now?"

Arena's circular course had brought us around into the wind and the boat's forward momentum took us up to the life preserver. Blaine fished it out of the water with the boathook as we went slowly by, and he reminded me that pulling my wife out would have been somewhat more complicated and that I would have plotted my approach so *Arena* would have been dead still in the water at the moment we reached the "victim."

"But that's something you'll learn," he said. "It took you a minute and forty-eight seconds. You'd better apologize to your wife." He handed me the sopping life preserver.

"I'm already trying to figure out how I could have gotten back faster," I said.

"Well, one thing you might have done is start the engine and motor around to her."

I felt, of course, like an absolute fool. As we sailed back toward the channel, though, Blaine very diplomatically talked about the things I'd done well and those that could "use some improvement." I was still deeply embarrassed about the person-overboard affair, but he told me not to worry. He was a forgiving boat owner.

"It happens to everybody," he said. "The way we did it, without warning, can be helpful practice. Sometimes you can be just sailing along and you pick up a life vest and throw it overboard, and you almost surprise *yourself*. It's very good practice. Chances are you won't forget the drill we just did."

He was quite right. I've never forgotten a moment of that minute and forty-eight seconds, and I've never sailed for a minute since then without making room back in a corner of my mind for a simple, effective plan of action—for a scenario that's waiting there, all ready to use, and that I hope I'll never have to use, for the moment when something or someone more valuable than a life preserver falls overboard.

CHAPTER NINE

Becoming a Sailor

As my experience grew, I found that I was taking sailing quite seriously. I was sailing as often as I could afford to, which was not nearly often enough, and when I was not sailing I was spending a good deal of time thinking about being on the water. My world had expanded, almost without my being aware of it. I had become, at least in mind, a sailor. How much of a sailor and how competent a sailor I would be were related, of course, to the skills I brought to it, but mostly they depended on practice—experience, study, training, time. And money, since sailing does not come for nothing.

The bits of experience have had a great cumulative effect, for learning one thing makes it easier to learn others. The matter of heeling is an example. Perhaps the thing that strikes the new or non-sailor's eye first when she sees a boat moving close-hauled through the water (and that strikes her even closer to the gut when she's actually aboard the moving boat) is the way the boat tips over to one side. Heel is a source of fear for new sailors, as well it should be. It seems to violate a lot of what we have been led to believe about balance. It looks like the very embodiment of a dangerous situation. It's pretty, but so are the pictures of hot-dog skiiers doing somersaults down the sides of mountains. To be sure, there is a heavily weighted keel down there, but *where*? The beginning sailor can't see the keel any more than the ancient sailors could see that Earth continued on around until it met itself, and that sailing beyond the horizon did not mean falling off into some fathomless void.

After a few sails during which the boat heels over quite far but neglects to capsize, the learning sailor incorporates that comforting experience into her knowledge of what happens when one goes sailing. This makes it possible to judge the degree of heel a lot more objectively, free from distracting concerns about imminent peril—to compare the boat's speed when there is a lot of heel to its speed when there is not a lot. That sets the stage for the discovery, exciting to some, that a lot of heel may *look* like a lot of speed, but it doesn't necessarily mean so. A lot of heel is for teenagers and other undiscriminating thrill-seekers.

To get where you're going in the fastest and most direct manner, you try to adjust your sails and tiller in such a way that the best possible balance exists between the boat and its immediate environment. That may or may not mean a considerable degree of heel, but chances are it will not. And the only way to learn that properly is to go out and learn it, at first hand, from the beginning. Some people learn it very quickly, while others take a long time. I was in the latter category. But now that the lesson has been learned, it is staying learned.

Very close to the lesson of the boat's heel, but on a slightly less physical and emotional level, is the matter of the line between excitement and danger. This is the sensation that I experienced when Blaine Liner and I took *Arena* out into the Neuse in winds that were a bit stronger than I had previously sailed in. Only experience can teach the sailor's mind when an exciting situation—and there are many of them in sailing—is dangerous and when it is exhilarating, and when, as is so often the case, the situation is changing from excitement into danger.

In my own experience, the search for this important line of demarcation has parallels in cross-country skiing. When I took up cross-country, there were few devotees of the sport in the eastern United States, and so there were few opportunities to learn how to do it right. The best advice seemed to be to find a golf course with snow on it and to fool around. But golf courses are among the most boring of mankind's creations, and I wanted to get out into the woods. In the East, that means relatively narrow and steep mountain trails that often are gullies filled with grapefruit-sized rocks. You can break your neck on them even when there isn't any snow at all. There was the added problem of very little snow of the right kind, with the result that I learned how to cross-country ski on terrain that was unsuitable and on a surface that was pretty much ice. I quickly developed a fear of going too fast on the skis, since there appeared to be no trustworthy way to stop or slow down.* All of this served to temper my enjoyment of cross-country until I managed one year to find some beautiful, rolling terrain with plenty of room for slowing down

---

* None of the books devoted serious attention to the problem of stopping, and no one I met on the trail seemed to have the answer. So one year when I was skiing in Stowe, Vermont, where they really know about such things, I paid out real money for a private lesson with an expert. (His sweater had "U.S.A." across the front, and he had that Olympic demeanor.) We skied along for a while, and eventually I asked The Question. "Best way I know is to sit down in the snow," he said. Which is what I had taught myself five years previously.

and running out at the bottoms of its hills, and that was practically deserted and covered with a deep layer of pristine powder. It was not on some Canadian glacier but a mile from my home, in Prospect Park, the 526-acre jewel in the center of Brooklyn that was laid out by landscape architects Frederick Law Olmsted and Calvert Vaux after they had done a fine job, but one less nearly perfect, on Central Park in Manhattan.

In my experiences with both cross-country skiing and sailing, the line between excitement and danger had to be established and observed and respected. Once that was done, I could afford to sit back and have a good time and enjoy what it was that I was looking for.

Each new sailing experience put another couple of bricks in the foundation I was building. Each one provided its own surprises and asked its questions, demanding that I come up with the answers. The answers could come only from what I had learned from others—in my now-copious reading on sailing and through mining others for their local knowledge—and from my own learning out on the water.

Once we and another couple chartered a boat on Long Island Sound. It was a brief charter, really little more than a deal to deliver the sailboat from its summer anchorage at a yacht club on the beautiful Connecticut coast to a marina farther west on the same coast, where it would be hauled from the water for the winter. It was a crisp and sunny October day, with a stiff breeze blowing that produced waves of a sort that I had never dealt with before. I suppose they were as much as four feet from tip to trough. I was glad that on this trip I was crew; the other couple was experienced in sailing the sound and in sailing this particular boat.

But by the time we got out of the harbor that changed.

My friends were suffering from unexpected attacks of back pain and motion sickness, and it fell to me to sail the boat. Experience, I recall, was jammed into a very tight space that day. The wind was howling, the waves were threatening, the rigging was totally unfamiliar to me, and the outboard motor didn't exactly calm our nerves: As we motored out into the deeper water the waves would toss the boat so that on every third wave or so the stern would be lifted high out of the water and the propeller, spinning against air, would shriek like a cat being disemboweled. We should have gone back but we didn't. Something in my embryonic experience, some previously forgotten brick down there in that shallow foundation, told me that things would get better if we could just get into the open water and get the sails up. And lo! it was true. As soon as the canvas was up the pitching stopped and the waves seemed to diminish, or at least to become tolerable. The utter silence of the four terrified people on board turned into gallows humor and then into ordinary chatter and, finally, into appreciation of the sharp autumn sights around us.

I also learned more that day than I could ever have imagined about leeway. I knew about leeway in principle: that when you're sailing close-hauled you appear to be traveling in a straight line but the wind and/or current may actually be setting you off at an angle to your course, and that such a diversion must be taken into consideration when plotting a course and, later, when steering it. But this was the first time I had ever seen and felt a graphic display of leeway. Long Island Sound is profoundly affected by current, and the wind was strong that day, and so we could observe the effects of leeway and compensate for them and—because our destination was not all that far away— we found out soon whether I was applying the right degree of correction. The next time I had an opportunity to build leeway into my steering, when I was sailing with some friends across Chesapeake Bay and took the helm for a while, I was able to do a more creditable job of it.

More sailing and more experience raised more questions and aroused more curiosity, and the answers sometimes were far more complicated than those I had dealt with before. I began nosing around, for instance, into navigation that is a bit more complex than the point-to-point piloting characteristic of coastal and lake sailing. I wondered and read about celestial navigation, and I spent some time trying to get my brain to understand the difference between great circles and rhumb lines.

A *great circle* is the shortest line between two points on the surface of a sphere. It is formed by drawing (mentally, if the sphere in question is Earth) a circle on the sphere through the two points, in such a way that the center of the circle passes through the center of the sphere. That's the shortest distance. So what? you may ask. Well, what's interesting is that much of our travel is not done by the great circle route, but by means of *rhumb lines*. If you're at Point A and want to get to Point B and you look at your chart and calculate the compass bearing from A to B, you are establishing a rhumb line course. It will differ from the great circle course because the chart is a flat, and therefore distorted, representation of the planet. Rhumb lines are fine for most sailing, but if you're planning a long trip—say, across the Atlantic Ocean—the great circle route would be the shorter distance. Plus it sounds neater than "rhumb line."

Will I ever master this information so that I will be able to use it? And if I *do* master it, *will* I ever be able to use it? The answer is, probably not. But for some reason that I don't quite understand, rhumb lines and great circles have become important to me.

Bowline

Some quite significant facets of sailing have resisted my best efforts at incorporating them into my repertoire. The bowline is among the handful of most important knots on a sailboat, and I still have trouble tying one. To tie a bowline (which is valuable because it is very strong, doesn't slip, and can be untied easily), you make a loop in a rope, then pass the free end through the loop and around the standing part and back through the loop. I am ashamed to say that about half my bowlines work only on the second attempt because I forget which side of the loop the free end goes through. This is simply a result of not enough practice. I really believe that if I could practice my bowlines sufficiently—a month-long cruise in the Caribbean in winter would probably do it—my embarrassment would be laid to rest.

With more sailing come more opportunities to observe other sailors on other boats and to work up fantasies about how the others enjoy the sailor's life. Often fantasies are easier to come by than hard facts, inasmuch as many of your observations are made while in motion: you and the others are almost literally two ships that pass in the night.

On that windy, exciting October day on Long Island Sound we saw several cruising boats that were obviously outfitted for the long haul, flying Canadian flags and headed south. The logical explanation was that these were Canadians who preferred warm wintertimes, and that they were headed for Florida or the Caribbean islands. I envied them as we passed, but I am not sure it was their destinations I envied, or even their finely-tuned and handsome boats. It seemed more to be the state of mind that they must have been enjoying just then: the knowledge that they were on a long and potentially exciting journey, one full of surprises; their self-sufficiency would be tested and they would be rewarded with sights and smells and emotions and, finally, memories that the rest of us might never have. I envied, I suppose, the *adventure* they were embarked on.

I have felt the same mixture of envy and admiration for the few round-the-worlders I've met. One couple and their cat came in to Oriental while I was there. The deck of their boat was covered with plastic jerry cans for drinking water; lines and extra lines were everywhere, and all of them seemed well-used. There was a self-steering device on the stern, a wind vane that could be set to handle the tiller so the sailors could take a break. The cat walked around as if he owned the place, and seemed not at all interested in visiting dry land. Inside the cabin, which had more than the usual complement of portholes and was light and airy, healthy-looking geraniums swung on chains from the overhead. The sailors, a young man and young woman, were deeply tanned and their hair had been bleached the same shade of blonde. And in their eyes one could see the adventure they were on.

Becoming a Sailor

Once again I had the feeling, this time in Florida. I was standing on the balcony of a hotel on Duck Key, which is about halfway between Key Largo and Key West, watching the sun rise out past Cuba. This time I had managed to spend a few days of *my* winter in a warm place, when I tagged along on my wife's business trip. Our room overlooked the open water and a circuitous canal that had been dug from it into the key's interior, and which was used as a protected boat passage to and from the center of the tiny island. Right on schedule, the sun quickly lifted its uppermost limb above the deep blue horizon. It was both as red as blood and as orange as a mandarin, and it was so enormous that I permitted myself the fantasy that it really was rising out of the warm southern sea, just over the horizon. I had seen several spectacular sunrises and sunsets since arriving in the Keys, but this was the clear winner. Then, out of the corner of my eye, I caught a smooth, gliding motion. A long, handsome, and no doubt very expensive sailboat was motoring quietly along the canal toward the open water. In the cockpit, her hands on a gleaming wheel, stood a woman, and on the foredeck was a man. They both wore bright yellow slickers that I knew the sun would soon allow them to stow below in the quarter berth. Their engine made practically no noise above a steady, well-oiled hum.

The man scanned the front of the hotel as they passed, and he saw me on the balcony and waved. I waved back. "Helloo," he called. He spoke in an almost conversational tone, yet I heard him clearly in the dawn quiet.

"Helloo," I replied.

"I wonder what the poor folks are doing today," he said, and waved again, and the sailboat moved on down the channel.

△ △ △

After sights and scenes such as these I found that chartering cruising sailboats was not only the logical next step, but also the necessary next one in my becoming a sailor.

Chartering is the renting of a boat for a period of time, often multiples of weeks, from the individual or company that owns it. I have never learned the precise difference between chartering and renting; like line and rope, it may be more a difference of vocabulary than anything else. But there is one component of boat chartering that is of supreme importance and that transcends the usual implications of renting. That is the assumption that the charterer, the person who is renting the boat, is competent to handle the boat under all the conditions that might be anticipated.

A lot of chartering is done, especially by people who have a sufficiency of money, on a captained basis. That is, a captain comes with the boat, perhaps with a crew and cook as well, and the charterers are passengers. They can, if they wish, help out with the sailing, all under the eye and tutelage of the captain. The other sort of chartering appeals to me: *bareboat* chartering. What you get for your fee is a bare boat (not literally; everything is there, or at least is supposed to be there, to sail her away; almost always there are pots and pans and utensils, life-saving equipment, and a lantern for anchoring overnight; and often there's a dinghy).

A charter can be an informal arrangement or it can involve the signing of complicated documents. It is a popular way for a boat owner to regain some of his investment in the boat during those times when he won't be needing it. And, in portions of the Caribbean and other places, chartering is a thriving business, with larger boats going for more than $1,000 a week (in 1982 dollars) during the winter season.

Chartering may be the only way that a sailor of limited means, and who isn't fortunate enough to have a mother-in-law like mine, has for getting out on the water. (The

$1,000-a-week rate is at the high end of the scale. Smaller boats may be chartered in less touristy places for considerably less than that.) There are other clear advantages, even for those who are not financially strapped: When you charter, you don't have to worry about continuous security or maintenance, and you don't have to pay year-round fees for maintenance, mooring, or docking. (Some boat owners haul their darlings out and stow them for the winter in their back yards, but in my case that would necessitate the removal of several neighbors' houses.) You are not tied to one geographical area. If you live and normally sail around Puget Sound and you're planning a trip to the East Coast and would like to give Chesapeake Bay a whirl, you don't have to sail your boat around Cape Horn or through the Panama Canal to get there. Nor are you restricted to one size and style of sailboat; with chartering you can dabble and experiment and shop around, perhaps even with an eye to the day when your ship really does come in and you can afford to buy it.

There are disadvantages, too, which any veteran of chartering can readily recite in great detail. We'll be getting to some of them shortly. But there do not always have to be problems; I can remember none at all when we chartered *Arena* again in the spring following our maiden voyage on Thanksgiving.

The weather was splendid, and this time I was considerably more confident of my ability to sail the boat. Because it was spring, the sun rose earlier and hung around longer than at Thanksgiving, and that meant more time to sail and explore. Eastern North Carolina's dogwood had already blossomed, but the woods and fields were congested with wildflowers and youthful green leaves at a time when the few brave trees and bushes back home were still trying to fight their way in the cold past the concrete and carbon monoxide. The mosquitoes were about as big as small watermelons, but their celebrated appetite for humans had not yet reached its summertime peak. We day-sailed the first day, went to the grocery store, talked with Andy about possible anchorages, and started our cruise on the following day. Andy lent us his dinghy, which we towed behind *Arena*, and we got going early, at what he referred to as "Oh-dark-thirty in the morning."

We ended up that first day in South River, although we didn't get there in a straight line but spent some time investigating both sides of the Neuse first. Once through the channel, we motored past Lukens and explored some of the river's ancillary creeks. We looked for the underwater artesian well Andy had told us about, but didn't find it. We *were* rewarded with an anchorage close to a sandy island, and we rowed over to it and swam along its beach before dinner. We had passed a few buildings, mostly vacation structures and some that were more in the category of fishing shacks, but at our anchorage that day we did not see another human being.

It was different on the following day. We sailed a few miles farther on toward the mouth of the Neuse and entered Turnagain Bay.

People back in Oriental had said the recesses of the bay made fine anchoring spots, but when I looked at our chart I saw that the channel at its entrance was covered—just barely, but nonetheless covered—by a purple circle whose center was at a place called Mulberry Point. And nearby, also in purple ink, was the legend:

Prohibited Area 204.55 (See Note A)

Note A, which was not far away, didn't offer much immediate help. Navigation regulations, it said, could be found in the regional edition of the *U.S. Coast Pilot*, a copy of which I should have had but didn't. I went with the local knowledge.

We motored, quickly and furtively, through the channel. I was relieved to see that the purple circle was not engraved on the very water itself. Once through the forbidden zone, we cautiously explored the depths of the bay and nosed into a couple of its sub-bays and creeks. We ran softly aground a couple of times in places where the chart swore we wouldn't. But the bottom was soft and yielding, and we needed only to throw the diesel into reverse to back off. Down toward the head of the bay, more than two miles from the entrance channel, there was something that fascinated me. The chart called it "Old Canal 5½ ft rep 1978," and it ran for about a mile through the marsh and led to an entirely different set of bays. *Arena*'s draft would allow it to traverse a five-and-one-half-foot-deep canal, but our recent multiple experiences at running a boat with a four-foot draft aground in water that was said to be twelve feet deep made me decide against such an expedition. So we picked a nice, wide section of the bay and dropped the hook. Clouds of seagulls, led by a fiery commander with distinctive markings, soon found us and pestered us for handouts. We provided them, word traveled instantly on the seagull grapevine, and approximately one million more of the birds arrived. We stopped casting our bread upon the waters and the gulls eventually went away. Or so I thought. I came out of the cabin with a cracker smeared with cheese in my hand and approximately two million of them appeared.

That evening toward dinnertime, as we were sitting in the cockpit marveling at the lack of mosquitoes and watching the sun prepare for a spectacular sunset, a single-engined, propeller-driven airplane flew low over the bay. It seemed to be scanning the immediate area of Mulberry Point, including the channel we had come through. Although I'm sure its pilot noticed us, there was no attempt to communicate with us. Then it flew away. Fifteen minutes later a lot of airplanes—military jets in camouflage—arrived, in a big hurry. And then the fireworks began.

The airplanes fired round after round of ammunition, including what appeared to be rockets, at a point on the ground maybe a mile away from us. As they made their passes, they turned and swooped away in what looked to be demonstrations of aerobatic ecstasy. There was silence for about ten minutes. Then another wave of planes came and demolished the land at Mulberry Point again. Finally, about an hour after it had all started, a rocket shot high into the air and a bright magenta flare descended slowly by parachute. There was silence again. The little propeller-driven plane returned, took a slow look around, and put-tered on back to where it had come from.

(It was not until later that I tried seriously to find out about Prohibited Area 204.55. I looked it up in my *U.S. Coast Pilot* and found that "The waters within a circular area with a radius of 0.5 statute mile having its center at latitude 35°00′30″, longitude 76°29′50′ [which appeared to be a very precise description of the purple circle centered on Mul-berry Point] will be used as bombing, rocket firing, and strafing areas." I could certainly testify to the accuracy of that. Continued the warning: "The areas shall be closed to navigation at all times except for such vessels as may be directed by the enforcing agency to enter on assigned duties. The areas will be patrolled and vessels 'buzzed' by the patrol plane prior to the conduct of operations in the areas. Vessels which have been inadvertently entered [*sic*] the danger zones upon being so warned shall leave the area immediately."

(Still, I wondered, why was there a marked channel into the bay if it was illegal to travel down it? Would it not be appropriate, as local knowledge had suggested, for a boat to pass quickly through the purple circle when there was no bombing going on? Note A promised the answers to these and other questions if I would but call the District Engineer, Corps of Engineers, in Wilmington, North Carolina. Which is what I did.

(The switchboard operator first transferred my call to the wrong department. Then I spoke at length with Navigation and Dredging, which said he didn't know the answer and referred me to Regulatory Functions. Regulatory Functions listened to my entire story and then informed me that he was concerned only with rules about construction. He referred me to the commander of the Fifth Coast Guard District in Portsmouth, Virginia. Note A, it seemed, told a lie.

(At that point I gave up and quit worrying about Prohibited Area 204.55. Since it was obvious that the regulators themselves didn't have the slightest familiarity with their own regulations, I was thrust back on my own common sense. It is in such ways that local knowledge is born.)

We learned a lot on that cruise, too, about the logistics of chartering. There is much about living on a sailboat, even for as short a period as a couple of days, that is vastly different from living anywhere else. Weather, which figures into much of our everyday thinking and planning only peripherally, is of supreme importance when you're cruising. If you are day-sailing, you come back to the dock at the end of a rainy, chilly day (if you went out into it in the first place), clean up, and head off to a restaurant that has a cheerful fireplace and an attentive audience for your tales of all the adversity through which you had to sail. If you are cruising from one anchorage to the next, the end of such a day means closing yourself up—with all the clothing and gear that got wet outside—inside a tiny, probably dark cabin. A sailboat cabin can get damp faster than a sponge and, once damp, takes a long time to dry out. The excitement and joy of being on an adventure can turn very quickly into depression and crankiness when you're damp and chilly all the time.

One way to minimize the problems of enforced, wet claustrophobia is to plan very carefully what you're going to take with you on the cruise, and then to cut that amount at least in half. You really need only something to keep you warm, something to keep you dry, and some things to change into when you're wet, along with devices such as books to keep you occupied. Having said that, I would add that I have never been able to pare it down that much, but I keep trying.

Provisions should be simple but rewarding. But, one might ask, rewarding for what? Isn't the cruise itself a reward? Is anybody forcing you to go sailing while the rest of the world slogs away at jobs it doesn't like? Of course it's a reward, and when you measure the actual amount of work done and energy expended in a day by a sailboat's worth of people, you come up with a figure that is considerably less impressive than comparable statistics for hiking, working at a desk job, or doing a Saturday shop at a large supermarket. But sailors always seem to end the day pleasantly exhausted, *as if* they had done a lot of highly productive work, and they always demand rewarding food.

The sort of reward is up to you, but it helps if it doesn't require ice. The ice chests on most boats I've seen have been poorly laid out and inadequately insulated. Marinas sell ice, of course, but who wants to plan a cruise to accommodate the stupid ice box? It's much better if you work out your meals so those requiring refrigerated food are consumed early in the trip and so no harm will occur if the ice runs out before the cruise is over. This may mean warm beer, but I have observed that sailors are infinitely adaptable in such matters. When the round-the-worlders put in at Oriental, somebody offered them a cold beer and they hesitated, declaring that they had gotten accustomed to the warm variety.

If you plan the cruise so you aren't dependent on ice, finding some along the way can be a pleasant surprise, in the same category with going to the produce market and discovering that the season's first asparagus is in. I once met a couple who were cruising south of Alexandria, Virginia, on the Chesapeake, the open Atlantic, and portions of the Intracoastal Waterway in a boat hardly bigger than the Ensign. They had a minimal amount of galley and cabin space, and there was no room for a large cooler. So they did without. I saw them in North Carolina, where a spur of the Waterway through the Great Dismal Swamp passes by the small community of South Mills. They were returning, beaming, from the general store with some canned food, peanut butter, bread, and two bags of ice. The ice, they said, was an unexpected treat.

Consider packaging when buying provisions for a cruise. On a cruising sailboat there are no convenient garbage pickups. Nor would anyone with the sense to read this book think of leaving his garbage behind on uninhabited islands, sandy beaches, unsandy beaches, or open water. Everything in the trash and garbage category must go into a garbage bag (a double bag is better), and the bag has to go somewhere (usually under one of the seats in the cockpit). It is to your great advantage to have to carry as little trash and garbage as possible, and that can mean repacking much of your food before the trip and discarding ahead of time the food manfacturers' wasteful and misleading packaging. People who go backpacking do this automatically.

Chartering, as I said before, sometimes has drawbacks. Once we arranged a formal charter through a marina (not Sailcraft) in eastern North Carolina. This time it was to be a thirty-foot C&C sloop—thirty feet being the largest boat I'd sailed so far, and C&C being a manufacturer with a reputation for building especially fine boats. Another couple was sharing the charter with us.

The boat's engine lacked the power to back us out of the slip. It had a blown head gasket. Surprisingly, this escaped the attention of the owner, who had brought it in from a cruise the day before. After much hemming and hawing with the chartering agent, during which time at least five tempers got good workouts, we were furnished with a thirty-three-foot sloop that is popular in the fancy charter trade. It was a great hulk of a boat that, I suspect, is perfect as a dockside vacation habitat for tourists in the Caribbean who want to go "sailing" without leaving the harbor. The cabin was as big as a volleyball court and as dark as a mausoleum. It took about half a hurricane to get the boat moving, and we had winds considerably less brisk than that. Thanks to a hydraulic device, turning her wheel gave me absolutely no sensation of steering the boat. In some ways the charter was a disaster.

Other chartering ventures have been less than satisfactory, too. One gentleman ran an ad offering for charter a boat that I especially had been hoping to sail, a wooden beauty called the Stone Horse, and a telephone call confirmed the boat's availability and its relatively low charter fee. I went to see it and meet the charterer. Unfortunately, the boat did not at the moment have a mast. And a preacher in Connecticut chartered us and some friends a nice little boat out of a nice little marina on Long Island Sound, and when we went to pick up the boat we found there was no key to the marina's gate or to its rest rooms, as well as a shortage of safety equipment on the boat. A telephone call to the preacher's secretary brought promises of relief that were not kept. We solved the first two problems by committing acts with adhesive tape on the marina's locks that might be construed as not wholly legal, and handled the second by including my own safety equipment, which I carry in anticipation of just such situations.

After the cruise the preacher failed to return to us the security deposit on his boat until many weeks passed and I started sending threatening letters by certified mail. He didn't know it, but when the check arrived I was about two Sundays away from walking into his church during the service and denouncing him in front of his congregation.

Experiences such as these have made me wonder if I wouldn't be doing would-be charterers a service by drawing up a list of things to have on hand when chartering a sailboat (at least on an informal basis from a private party). It would include a lawyer (for interpreting the agreement); an officer of the law or rent-a-cop (for enforcing it); a typewriter, stationery, and certified mail forms (for serving notice, threatening, etc.); an anchor light (especially if the owner says there's one aboard, a dead tipoff that there isn't); a lead line, which is a length of line with a weight at one end and feet or fathoms marked off along its length (for boats that are said to have depth finders); flares, life vests, floating cushions, and other safety equipment; a kerosene or butane stove (to replace the stock alochol stoves, which never work properly); a sharp all-purpose knife to replace the dull absurdity you'll find in the galley; a supply of water (the thirty-three-foot, luxurious cruising sloop had a shower, of all things, but its tank held about enough water to chase down two aspirin); your own toilet; shock cords (these heavy elastic cords with hooks at the end are very valuable for doing a dozen different jobs, and boat owners never leave theirs on board); and a basic tool set, including a screw driver, plastic tape, and Vise-Grip pliers.

The list is partly an exaggeration, but not all that much of one. Anybody who sails must expect to encounter the unexpected, but ideally the encounters take place on the water and out in nature, not just outside locked marina toilets and with boat owners whose boats are not in sailing condition.

But even with the drawbacks, chartering is a useful and effective access to sailing, especially for the person who is in the process of becoming a sailor, who wants to sample it all, and who still hasn't decided what sort of sailing he wants to do—and especially for those of us who don't have the money to own a boat. Besides, there are good sides to even the bad experiences. Our dealings with the thirty-three-foot monstrosity let us scratch it off our life list of sailboats we'd ever want to own or to sail again. And when we turned the boat in I asked the charterer to write a letter attesting to my ability to sail her—and got one proclaiming my "competency in handling a boat of this size and characteristics"—a document that will be helpful next time I want to charter a larger boat. Best of all, when we were entering a river for our anchorage the first night out in the hulk we were greeted and escorted by what must have been three dozen porpoises, arching their shiny, handsome backs out of the water in a mockery of the tublike shape of our boat and making us very happy.

The debacle of the preacher's charter did nothing to lessen my interest in sailing Long Island Sound. I know that someday I will find a Stone Horse *with* a mast. I want to charter a boat in Oriental with a very short draft and sail her carefully through Prohibited Area 204.55, full of local knowledge and my new-found appreciation of just how inadequate official knowledge can be, and find that Old Canal 5½ ft rep 1978, go down it, and see what's on the other end.

It is through chartering—sailing a variety of other people's boats in a thus-far modest variety of places and situations—that I have accumulated the experiences that lead me to believe that I have become a sailor. I know (and it is a joyous knowledge, not the knowledge of apprehension that I once had, back when I could not read the wind and didn't know how dangerous a heeling sailboat was or wasn't) that there are new experiences, new things to learn, just around the corner. Or at least just around the corner when I've scraped up enough money and stolen enough time to go sailing again.

I don't particularly want to find myself in a storm so severe that I'll have to shorten sail drastically, but I know that I'm shy on that sort of experience and I've got to learn, sooner or later. Most and best of all, I know that there are all kinds of nooks and crannies of the natural world that can be seen best by sailboat, and I want to see as many of them as I can before it's all over.

CHAPTER TEN

Sailing and the Planet

A lot of what has been said here about sailing may make it sound more like work than play. Learning a strange vocabulary, defying the penetrating stares of the dock committee, keeping proper track of the flashing greens and quick-flashing reds, maintaining a lookout for prohibited areas (not to mention rocket attacks), remembering the difference between variation and deviation—it all may sound very much like sailing falls considerably short of a joyous, carefree afternoon out in the sun and wind and spray.

Of course, it is not all work, or mostly work, or even very much work. Sailing is fun, and sailing is rewarding in ways that are even better than fun. Energy, both mental and physical, is indeed expended, but the calories that get burned and the neurons that get exercised produce the warmth of pleasant tiredness, not nerve-frazzled exasperation. Sailing promotes mental health rather than endangers it. I could see that sailing might be "work" for someone who had an investment in it so immense that he felt he *had* to sail. The problem is a common one among people who have so much money and emotion tied up in vacation homes that they have ceased to enjoy them. But that need not be a problem for the sailor, especially if he is cunning enough to be poor enough to not afford his own boat.

The rewards are multitudinous. In my own brief time as a sailor, and as one who doesn't get to sail nearly as much as he'd like to, I have been amazed at the quality and diversity of the payoffs.

For one thing, sailing is something you don't have to be under thirty and a born athlete to enjoy or to do well. In fact, the older you are the better you can be at it, because it is experience, not youthful vigor, that counts in sailing. While your muscles might not be as supple and well-toned as a teen-ager's, the neurons will have ripened through aging, and you may even find yourself dispensing rations of *wisdom* every now and then when you're deciding, say, whether it's time to shorten sail, or whether to make it home in one very long tack or in several shorter ones. You find that, far from being dead or terminally atrophied, your memory welcomes with touching gratitude information that is truly important, not just the junk mail you usually send it. Once you learn to sail—really learn it, through trial and error, frequent failure and occasional embarrassment and occasional triumph—you don't lose it. It is like the proverbial process of learning to ride a bicycle. Once yours, it is yours forever.

One summer when I went to Petoskey I realized that it had been almost eleven months since I had sailed. I rowed out to the Ensign, raised the sails, and went. I remembered it all. The feelings for and of the wind, the boat, and the lake were all there. They didn't *come back*; they had been there, in my head and eyes and arms and hands, all along.

Sailing scours the rust from your mind better than most things I know. The oxidation builds up quickly and thickly

these days: the constant flow of bills from people who naturally expect to be paid; the phone calls from stores trying to
sell you service contracts on junk that fell apart a year ago;
an increasing dependence on technological inventions that
don't solve the old problems and that create new ones; the
daily reinforcement of your suspicion that things are getting
worse; the equally frequent insults to our intelligence by
the politicians we've elected—everyone has her and his own
depressing list. The rust gets thicker, and it obscures the
truly important things from your attention, and if you're
not careful you find yourself paying more attention to the
rust than to the rest of your existence. A scowl etches itself
into your face, and when you walk down the sidewalk little
kids cringe in terror and cats wisely cross the street.

But when you're sailing, the rust disappears. Sailing
has a marvelous capacity for separating what's really significant from what isn't. When you're sailing, you must put all
the extraneous things aside and concentrate on the handful
of truly important things: on today, and on now, and on
how to get from Point A to Point B safely. When you do get
to Point B, and then to home, the bills and politicians and
patches of rust will still be there. But you'll be able to view
them in a more realistic way, and maybe to cope with them
in a less desperate manner.

Not only does sailing clean your mind like a southern
thunderstorm cleans the thick summer air; it also opens
your head up to thoughts and concepts that may be new to
you or that you may have investigated before and abandoned as too difficult to cope with. In my own case, this
was dramatically demonstrated in the area of mathematics.

For some reason, my brain has always gone into a
trance when confronted by matters of mathematics. From
high school on, it seemed incapable of making the short
jump between reality and the symbols of reality that are

manipulated in geometry, algebra, calculus, and all their nephews and second cousins. It wasn't that I couldn't add and subtract or carry on transactions that involved numbers. It was just that my mind was unable or unwilling to grasp, and then to remember, the workings of equations with lots of *a*s and *b*s and *(a + b)*s in them. It was the same with triangles, circles, spheres, and all the other shapes that demanded to have their volumes calculated, their angles measured, their πs sliced. As I fell further and further behind my classmates, I shrugged defensively and declared that, just as some people don't have finely-tuned senses of color, musical tone, or depth, the "mathematical side" of my brain wasn't properly developed. And so I concentrated on words instead of numbers. In college, where a couple of semesters of math were required even of English majors, they had to create a special class for me and a handful of similarly gifted students, complete with compassionate teacher and custom-written curriculum. It didn't work. The teacher deteriorated daily before our eyes, and there was nothing any of us could do about it.

I would have spent the rest of my life avoiding mathematics as if it were an allergy, in the way that some of my friends must avoid woollen clothing or house cats, had it not been for sailing. As mentioned before, an evolving sailor can go in any of a number of directions, be they ocean traveler or occasional Sunfisher, and still be a sailor. But if the direction points toward cruising—exploration, searching out the recesses and alcoves of the natural world that still remain defiantly hidden from the Interstates and the burger joints—the sailor must learn a few things about navigation, and that means mathematics.

All of a sudden I realized that those rules about triangles, the ones I was supposed to have learned back in the ninth grade but didn't, were very helpful in getting from one place to another in a sailboat. Using your compass and your eyeballs and a little mathematics, you could measure the angle between your course line and a daybeacon or point of land and throw in a few other numbers and assumptions and come up with a pretty good idea of where you were!

By measuring your angle to an object and then figuring the distance you travel until the object is directly abeam, or perpendicular to you, you could deduce the distance to the object. Or by fooling around a bit with the height of a known object (such as a lighthouse) that has just appeared on the horizon, you can determine your distance to that object. It's simple. The equation is:

$$D = 1.144\left(\sqrt{Ho} + \sqrt{He}\right)$$

where *D* is the distance from you to the object in nautical miles, *Ho* is the height of the object in feet (obtained from a chart or other nautical publication), and *He* is the height of your eye above the water, also measured in feet. The *1.144* does the equation's magical work by applying the curvature of the earth to the other values. For example:

You're sailing on one of the Great Lakes and your chart tells you there's a 62-foot-tall lighthouse over to the west. You figure your eye is 7.5 feet above the water. You train your binoculars on the horizon, and at the moment the top of the lighthouse pops up, you work the equation. The square root of 62 is 7.87; add that to 2.74 (the square root of 7.5) to get 10.61, and multiply that by 1.144. You are 12.14 nautical miles from the lighthouse. If you can obtain another line of position (from another navigational aid, or perhaps from a later observation of the same lighthouse), you will have established a fix and you'll know pretty well where you are.

So, after almost a quarter century of neglect—more

than neglect: abandonment—the numbers started meaning something to me. They became valuable. I never really gave a damn about where the two trains, one leaving Chicago at 60 miles an hour and the other leaving Washington at 45, would meet. I failed to appreciate the value in poor Johnny's eternal calculations concerning apples and oranges. As far as I could tell, these were thinly-disguised efforts to make something that was inherently and basically useless sound as if it had some importance. Now, on the lower Neuse River or the rocky Connecticut side of Long Island Sound, it became important to me. I loved it.

I bought a programmable calculator and spent hours learning how to work it. Then I bought another one, infinitely better, a real little computer that fits in my pocket and that is called the Hewlett-Packard 41C. I learned how to write programs for it. Just for fun, I dreamed up one that takes the time between lightning's flash and its sound and spews out the bolt's distance from me in nautical miles, statute miles, kilometers, yards, and feet, all corrected, of course, for the ambient temperature. I wrote another one that reduces the distance-to-object-at-horizon equation to a few taps of the keypad. The program, which I named "Horize," looks like this:

```
01◆LBL "HORIZE"
02 "HT OBJ FT?"
03 PROMPT
04 SQRT
05 "HT EYE FT?"
06 PROMPT
07 SQRT
08 +
09 1.144
10 *
11 "N.M. OFF="
12 ARCL X
13 AVIEW
14 .END.
```

When you run "Horize" using the heights of object and eye mentioned earlier, the program works out the equation like this:

```
01◆LBL "HORIZE"
        "HT OBJ FT?"
                PROMPT
HT OBJ FT?
        62.00    RUN
                 SQRT
        7.87    ***
        "HT EYE FT?"
                PROMPT
HT EYE FT?
        7.50    RUN
                 SQRT
        2.74    ***
                  +
       10.61    ***
                1.144
                  *
       12.14    ***
        "N.M. OFF="
                ARCL X
                AVIEW
N.M. OFF= 12.14
                .END.
```

[Those unfamiliar with the Hewlett-Packard way of doing things may be confused by the order in which the calculations are carried out. That's because the machine uses Reverse Polish Notation (invented by the logician J. Luksiewicz), which means it adds 2 and 2 not by saying "2 + 2 = 4" but by saying "2, 2, +". The machine doesn't even have an equals key.]

Although there were no ocean voyages on my immediate horizon, so to speak, I obtained a cheap plastic sextant and amused my neighbors by taking noon sun shots from the roof of my house. Because a horizon is required if the sextant is to furnish an accurate angle with the sun, I had to compromise. The Lower Bay of New York City is visible from my roof, and it extends back to a sort of quasi-horizon that is nine-tenths New Jersey air pollution, but it was in the wrong direction for midday shots. So I declared that a certain roof on a certain brownstone about eight blocks south of my house was the horizon. My early shots worked out amazingly well, for a beginner; the mapmakers had misplaced Brooklyn by only about forty-five miles.

I went down to the harbor to a secret little waterfront place I know (no easy trick; you have to wade through tons of garbage and debris and find your way through a fence that some arrogant government agency has thrown up to separate the people from their heritage) and took a sextant reading on the World Trade Center, an object of known height. Then, using a variation on the "Horize" equation, I figured its distance from me. It was one and a half nautical miles, exactly the distance I measured later on a chart. While I was taking the shot a wrinkled, leather-faced man with a cane walked by, stopped, watched, waited until I had my reading, and then said:

"For forty years I take the shot of the sun on the ship, a freighter, every day, and sometimes the stars too. This is the first time I ever see the shot taken on the city." I explained what I was trying to do. This seemed to delight the man, for, he said, "Too many people around now who don't know even what the sextant is." He said this, mind you, to someone who five years before could not have articulated the difference between a hypotenuse and a hippopotamus.

So when you start to become a sailor you find, to your great amazement, that you are transcending the person you thought you were. There was a time when you were certain you would never be able to tell which way the wind was blowing, but one day you broke through that frustrating layer of ignorance. And that was just the beginning.

There are other forms of personal growth, too. Sailing taught me not to inflict my reverse snobbery on sailing people, even those who speak of "Yachting." It has caused me to walk a little taller, a little more confidently, when I'm around the water, as if I shared something with all the other sailing people through history. And it has taught me that there is no such thing as "knowing how to sail." It is an endless, ongoing process, with always an abundance of new things to learn, new places to discover, new adventures to have. Sailing increases and sharpens your appreciation of beauty, not only the beauty of the natural world of the water and sky but also that of sailing itself. A well-executed tack or jibe can be an act of beauty, almost in the category with a well-executed ballet step, as is an approach to the dock or mooring that brings you to a perfect stop so you just reach over and attach your lines. A well-built sailboat (they are among the few things that are still put together by hand) is a piece of living, working sculpture. And there are few sights more beautiful than a distant sailboat under sail.

This last invader of your emotions works two ways. I have looked out on the water from land—onto the Atlantic Ocean from the shorefront drive in Newport, Rhode Island; onto the Pacific from the promenade, jammed with roller skaters, in Santa Monica; onto Lake Michigan from a bluff on a narrow highway south of Charlevoix—and have seen a set of sails, translucent and as airy white as down, far on the horizon, as if the world really were flat and the boat were skimming along its very edge, the sails straining with wind, the angle of the mast showing the drive and power and excitement of the voyage; and I have been moved almost to tears of joy. And there have been other times, days when it was cold or rainy or when the wind was maybe a little too puffy for sensible people, when I have been sailing by myself and have felt lonely on the water. I have seen no other boats, and I sometimes have wondered if everybody else knew something I didn't know, and maybe *I* should have stayed in, too. And then my eye has caught another set of sails and I have been instantly comforted, reassured.

I suspect the sailors in the other boat were just as pleased to see my sails. Solitary sailors are like solitary backpackers and beachwalkers. They don't like too many people around them; that is one reason they go places by themselves. But they are cheered when they cross paths with other solitary walkers from time to time, or when they see another line of footprints along the sandy beach. It is good to know there are others out on the enormous planet with us, for we are not really meant to be solitary people at all.

Just as I learned to feel the wind and to use the elementary tools of the navigator's art, I started learning other things. The natural world opened up for me more than I thought possible—and as a lover of hiking and canoeing I had not been any stranger to the natural environment before. Sailing brought me face-to-face with weather, with clouds, with the nighttime sky. I embraced these parts of nature eagerly, excitedly now, seeing them through completely new eyes, just as I had come to see the laws of right triangles and cosines in a totally different way. Of course, I had had a speaking acquaintance with weather and skies before. But now it was an intense, devoted relationship. These things were valuable to me now; they enriched my life.

It was a lot like my introduction to cross-country skiing. I had never cared much for winter sports—never even thought about them, actually. I grew up on the South's coastal plain, where snow, on those rare occasions when it did fall, almost always was melted by lunchtime. When I moved to the North it was to New York City, where snow is regarded not as a thing of beauty but as yet another nasty trick played on hard-boiled New Yorkers by a nature that refuses to understand that the urbanity and sophistication of New Yorkers places them somewhere above the environment. In order to demonstrate nature's folly to her, New Yorkers see to it that their dogs turn a fresh snowfall an instant yellow-brown, and then they dump their garbage in it. So snow in my adopted home does not produce much in the way of picture-postcard New England scenes.

I knew all along (because I had previously seen snow that wasn't yellow-brown) that winter wasn't really like that, but I did little to verify that knowledge. Like lots of other people, I locked myself inside my house from the time of the pumpkins until the appearance of the crocuses. Then I got a pair of touring skis and it all changed. The winter opened up for me; it became as exciting for me as any other season, a time to be enjoyed and anticipated.

Largely because of sailing, I think, all of the seasons became more important and more delightful for me. If you sail one body of water often you find that it offers an especially stirring way to observe the changes in the seasons. You realize, as you sometimes aren't able to in the big city, that the seasons don't just switch on and off at the precise moments dictated by Earth's angle to the Sun and as reported in all the almanacs; but that the process is a powerful, unstoppable, constantly (but sometimes imperceptibly) moving progression from birth to rich, lush life, to decline, to a state that looks very much like death, to mourning, and then to birth again. Any stretch of water, no matter how big or small, can become your own version of Thoreau's Walden Pond or Concord River, and once it becomes yours, its seasons belong to you too.

To me, Walloon has always been in the process of becoming autumn. That is because I have been there mostly in the late summer, and I am from a much more southern part of the country, and autumn comes early in the Michigan north, up there halfway to the Pole. Even before Labor Day they start taking in the docks, and the kids from the marinas come in motorboats and tow the sailboats and houseboats down the lake for winter storage. You watch this from the water on one of your last sails (you cannot be sure, for the weather may make it the last one of the season), and you look up for a moment and are astonished to see that the leaves of the trees along the shore have started to turn.

I will remember eastern North Carolina, though, as always moving toward warmth, toward summer. It is a place of balmy warm winds up from the tropics, of rich dogwoods and fragrant pines and fat, lazy snakes and huge, sharp-eyed, searching hawks, and the surest sign of summer: the late afternoon thunderstorms that sometimes build mile-high columns of charcoal-gray sky before they release their awesome energy. And everyplace else that I sail I learn a little more of the seasons; it all goes into my memory and experience and waits for its place in my future.

Sailing has taught me to appreciate the daytime sky—to learn to read its clouds and wind direction so that I might predict what the remainder of my cruise (or the rest of my afternoon on a Sunfish) will be like. One does not turn that appreciation off at the end of the period of time spent on a boat, but carries it over into every day, every glance at the sky. Even as I walk through the filthiest of Manhattan's streets, or along the most extravagantly manicured of its avenues, I find myself aware of where the wind is coming from and what the sky is like, incorporating that into my own personal weather forecast.

Because I could not help but fantasize about the longer voyages, whether or not I will ever really be able to take them, I became a watcher of the night sky, too. Long before I got my plastic sextant and tried pointing it at Polaris, I was lying flat on my back on a lawn chair at Petoskey, and sometimes lying on the floor of the Ensign's cockpit at her mooring, and matching the patterns I saw up there with those of the sky chart I had bought.

At moments such as those, you cannot help but become aware of a couple of facts. One is that time is truly very relative. There is no better way in all the world to comprehend that than to spend an hour or two bucking a strong current or tacking endlessly in order to get to a destination a few miles away, and meanwhile to look up and see a commercial jetliner streaking across the sky, going halfway to the other side of the country in the time it takes you to reach the next daybeacon—and to know that, regardless of the conclusion that some realists might draw, your method is the finer one. Or to row out to a sailboat that you last sailed the day before yesterday, climb aboard and discover that in your brief absence one purportedly insignificant spider has stitched an enormous coverlet for the cockpit and is now working on the standing rigging.

The second fact is one that may be apparent only to those of us who have hit middle age. It has to do with death. Should it be perhaps not surprising that this much-delayed interest in the intricacies and wonders of nature; this sudden discovery of the nighttime sky, and this absorption in the stars and planets and their movements and the lone navigator's relationship to them; this new devotion to learning how to get safely from one place to another and to do it yourself, on a very big amount of water in a very small boat, equipped with little more than the instruments that were used by the most ancient of mariners—should it be not surprising that all these probes into an area of great mystery and uncertainty come to a focus at a time when the end of life is not the utter impossibility that it was when one was a teenager, or the very distant likelihood that it was when one was thirty, but now a clear inevitability? Is it too silly or melodramatic to wonder if one is actually rehearsing, getting one's affairs in order for, the final, mysterious voyage?

I sat at the picnic table by the water in Petoskey one day, working out the sextant shot I had just taken. My sister-in-law, a very bright lawyer, walked by. "What are you doing?" she asked.

"Learning to use the sextant," I replied.

"But you don't use the sextant in the kind of sailing you do, do you?"

"No," I said.

"Are you *going* sailing where you'll use it?"

"Not anytime soon."

"So why are you doing it?"

"I don't know," I said.

Chief among sailing's payoffs, then, is that it helps to make you a part of the planet and, if you're willing to be sentimental about it, part of the universe. It also produces environmentalists in great profusion.

More clearly in sailing than in any other avocation I know, the lesson is made with undeniable clarity that human beings must exist in balance with nature, and not at nature's expense. And when you have sailed a while, one of your more rewarding discoveries may be that you are working out in your own mind your own personal definition of what the balance should be. We are all "environmentalists" of one sort or another. No one, not even the worst of the strip miners, is so set against the forces of nature that he or she refuses to have any association at all with the natural world. Each of us subscribes to a notion of just how the equation between humans and nature should be divided.

Some give nature very little weight and humans very much. Some see humans as relatively insignificant in the big scheme of things, of no more or less real *value* to the planet than an ant or a grasshopper or the spider who weaves a web on the sailboat.

Arguments over the equation have become one of the most important issues of the 1980s—and, because the issue is so important and our response to it so full of implications for the long-range future of Earth, quite possibly of the decades and centuries to follow. After an era in which the equation was tipped slightly in favor of the environment, we have entered a period in which the people who run our government are advocates of a different form of "balance": one in which nature is deemed to exist solely for the entertainment and utilization of mankind, like the commercially-raised chickens that are scientifically hatched, grown, fed, slaughtered, and packaged in huge factories and that never see daylight or walk upon the ground. Some government officials even say that nature is there only to sustain "civilization" as it awaits its summons to a higher, spiritual form of life, and that therefore there is no need to worry about the long run, the effects of the strip mines and polluted oceans. For both sides in this argument the issue has become one of almost religious intensity and significance.

I do not see how a sailing person could possibly be one of those who views nature as our servant, as disposable as the superfluous paper bag that comes around a fast-food hamburger. The sailor is too close to the truth, too close to nature, for that. The sailor owes not only his and her enjoyment and satisfaction to nature, but also his and her continued existence. That may not be clear to someone sitting in an executive office at the Interior Department or the Pentagon or a multi-national conglomerate or a paper mill, but it is exquisitely clear to the sailor out on the water.

Something reverential happens to a person when he

leaves the "civilized" world, with all its No Fault insurance and disclaimers of responsibility, its 800 numbers and hot lines and credit cards, and sets out on a place where self-reliance and accountability are what is ultimately important. When you are on the water, you are responsible for your own wake. It is one of the more basic of the rules of the water, and it used to be a fundamental precept of civilized society. You do damage; you pay for it. This means if you're motoring too fast down a narrow channel and the wake from your boat slams a docked boat against a pier and damages it, you are responsible. It is elemental, a logical extension of common decency. But it also means— and sailing people recognize and understand this far better than most others—that whatever damage we inflict on our environment, we or our children will eventually pay for. It is abundantly obvious to any sailor that only a fool tries to fight nature.

But neither is the sailing person likely to be one of those who would lock up nature, declare it off-limits to all human travel and use, seal it in a bell jar and put it in a museum and show it only by appointment. Humans can exist in a proper balance with nature that does neither the humans nor the environment any harm, and that in fact does them both a lot of good. Because they enter this balance every time they go out on the water, sailing people understand this more readily than others.

In this sense, sailing is likely to make one who is inclined toward protecting the environment a more optimistic person than before. For sailing allows you to see, close up and at water level, not only the corrupting urban water-fronts and the tacky riverside housing developments but also examples of nature's great resiliency and magnificent perseverance.

Once, when we were anchored in South River, off the abandoned fishing town of Lukens, I woke early and crept past my sleeping wife out the cabin and onto the deck to watch the sunrise. The water was calm in the dawn, and the seagulls were calling, but it was not with the anxiety of the evening before. Now it was almost as if they were speaking morning greetings to each other, mindful as humans are that some of their number were still sleeping and others still groggy—small, almost whispered certifications that we have got through another night.

At 6:30 someone from one of the houses on the other side of the creek, a building that I could hardly even see, cranked up a large engine on a small boat and started off across the water. I could tell that it was a fisherman's boat, one made for working the crab line and not for fancying around with water skiiers. The sound of the motor went on for a very long time, long after the boat had passed through the creek's mouth into the broad Neuse. And I found that the sound of this manmade contraption, this collection of metal parts that creates unmuffled sound and burns irreplaceable fuel and leaves harmful things in the air and little rainbows of oily pollution on the water whenever it stops, didn't bother me at all, even at dawn. It was part of the watery life, part of the environment of the place, and not a hurtful part at all.

And I shall never forget what happened when we took the Laser out into Jamaica Bay. This was the day we rented the board boat in New York City and learned that when the wind is behind you and you let the sail get ahead of the mast, you capsize.

Before we learned that, we sailed for an hour or so among the islands and marshes of the bay—Silver Hole Marsh, East High Meadow, Winhole Hassock. The fact that we were not in the wilderness was constantly apparent in the arrival and departure of jets at Kennedy Airport, whose runways were less than a nautical mile away. In and out they screamed, at times so low that I involuntarily braced myself in the boat, assuming that anything that big and loud and close by would surely shake the water below and anything that was on it.

The airplanes were not all. The bay is used by commercial shipping, and several freighters passed nearby, low in the water with their cargoes of oil and aviation fuel. Whenever we sailed near solid land we would see nasty-looking pipes leading into the bay from the shore and civilization's ancient sewage system. In New York, as in many others among the older coastal cities, it is not safe to assume that those pipes have been replaced by more modern, environmentally acceptable systems.

We were carrying some lunch in a tightly-closed plastic bag, and when an island with a sandy beach appeared before us we could hardly resist. It was well out of the channels used by freighters, and it was surrounded by sand, which made beaching the boat and walking ashore more attractive and easier. The island has no name on *Nautical Chart 12351, Jamaica Bay and Rockaway Inlet*, but it is important nonetheless. It serves as one of the supports for the tracks of a subway line, the one that carries the "A" train from miles away, in the Bronx, through Harlem to the seediest and most dangerous of all the subway stations in Times Square, then downtown and into Brooklyn and into Queens and finally, when it emerges from its tunnel and begins to run above ground, out past Kennedy Airport and across the water to a terminal on the Rockaways.

So we sat on the beach on the unnamed island in the midst of all the pollution and poverty and development and waste, and we gazed at it all and ate our lunch. All around us in the water and scattered along the beach were the two by-now standard indicators that civilization was nearby: shards of styrofoam and dozens of the indestructible plastic applicators for tampons. The tiny sailboat was on the beach in front of us, its one sail hanging free in the wind, looking like a colorful advertisement for some delightful Caribbean island. It was the only sail we saw that day, and that made our accomplishment all the more delightful. It was like beating a small part of the system.

An "A" train clattered by on its tracks a hundred yards away. Our sail must have been a surprise to its passengers. The train was ugly-looking and covered with graffiti, a rolling, squeaking, tattered pestilence, and in the sunlight and open space it looked much smaller and less important than it did when it was screaming its way through a subway tunnel.

To our left, in the greater distance, a strange-looking aircraft with white wings and body moved swiftly down a runway and gained the air long before its high-pitched sound reached us. Once airborne, it passed over us not far away, rising rapidly. Its delta-shaped wings and articulated beak-nose showed it was a Concorde, the expensive super-sonic passenger plane that ferries people from the United States to Europe and back at record speed but at great cost to the environment. The plane was, in that respect, incredibly ugly. But as it flew away to London it was also incredibly beautiful.

The "A" train rattled out of sight, and a freighter passed far away, carrying fuel to a city that already is too polluted to be cleaned up. The water we had sailed in lapped higher against the boat's hull and threatened to float it away. The tide was rising.

I waded out to pull the sailboat in closer, walking carefully because I feared what might be on the bottom of a body of water that was within sight of the skyscrapers of the most self-centered city on earth. And then I noticed the horseshoe crabs.

There were thousands of them. They were all over the shallow water, scooting along the sandy bottom, darting past the jetsam of society, avoiding the insoluble plastic detritus. Some were heading off into deeper water and others were just arriving. They were in all sizes, some as big as dinner plates and others the size of saucers. They were in varying colors, but almost all were shades of brownish-red. As they skimmed the sand, their long tail spikes swung from their tough but brittle shells.

They seemed oblivious to me, the boat, the "A" train, the Concorde, the debris in the water, the City of New York, and the argument about the balance between human beings and nature. In the midst of all this ugliness and pollution, in this stretch of what I had taken to be poisoned, burned-out water, thousands of horseshoe crabs were enthusiastically, lustily celebrating life by mating with each other.

With what only could have been delight, they climbed over, under, and onto each other, clinging tightly and scouring round depressions in the sand, and proving that nature exists for the occasional convenience of horseshoe crabs as well as humans, and also proving that there is absolutely no section of the planet that can be written off as too far gone.

Clove hitch

Sources

There is no end of written information on how, where, and what to sail. The offerings are so abundant, in fact, that the beginning sailor is likely to become quite confused when he or she sets out to learn more. Many of the books that are aimed at the learner almost equal fad diet books when it comes to exaggerated claims. None of them can be expected to provide everything the sailor needs (though some come surprisingly close), and so one's bookshelf is likely to develop quite a sag.

The most substantial resource, of course, is one's own experience. But a good selection of books and periodicals, combined with experience and local knowledge gleaned from more experienced sailors, will help a lot to prepare the part-time mariner for rewarding and safe journeys.

The list that follows contains those publications that I have found most helpful.

SAILING IN GENERAL   One of the major faults of sailing books is that they usually are written by experts who know their subject terribly well and who assume that the reader understands something when quite likely the reader doesn't. Time-Life Books has always tried to avoid that trap in its several series on everything from sewing to art to foods of the world. Volumes in the Time-Life Library of Boating that appeal to sailors are no exception to this tradition. The language is clear and the graphics are excellent. My favorites are the volumes titled *Navigation, Seamanship, Cruising,* and *Cruising Grounds.*

The New Glenans Sailing Manual, translated by James MacGibbon and Stanley Caldwell (Boston: Sail Books, 1978), is very comprehensive and full of solid information on sailing theory. The book was compiled by the staff of a famous sailing school in France. Among other things, however, it contains the shocking advice that "drinking sea water does not have the dire consequences . . . as was once believed." And as is still believed by all the experts I ever heard of.

Stephen Colgate, author of *Fundamentals of Sailing, Cruising, and Racing* (New York: W. W. Norton, 1978), runs a sailing school of his own. His book is quite comprehensive, although I suspect his heart is really in racing. The book recycles a lot of material from his *Colgate's Basic Sailing Theory* (New York: Van Nostrand Reinhold, 1973), so if you have one you don't need the other. Explanations of boat stability and sail trim are excellent in both books.

Alice and Lincoln Clark's *The ABCs of Small Boat Sailing* (Garden City, N.Y.: Dolphin Books, 1963) is a fine little paperback with most of what you need to know about sailing, arranged alphabetically, and with illustrations wherever words aren't enough. The book is small enough to take along on a sailing expedition.

Sailing Illustrated, by Patrick M. Royce (Newport Beach, California: Royce Publications, 1956 and later editions), is also pocket-sized and useful in a hurry, but it contains some of the most ungrammatical assaults on the English language that I have ever witnessed. Many helpful illustrations.

It helps if you can identify and visualize sailboats other than the ones you're familiar with, especially if you charter boats and want to see what you're getting into. One way to do this is through the annual *Sailboat & Equipment Directory*, published by Sail Publications, Boston. Sailboats are listed in order of length, with basic information, a descriptive paragraph (often obviously written by the manufacturer), sometimes a cabin blueprint, and a little drawing of the boat.

EXPERIENCES   There are a lot of books by folks who have single-handed around the world or around Cape Horn or elsewhere, and many of them seem to have been written by marvelous sailors who are not marvelous writers. Joshua Slocum's *Sailing Alone Around the World* and *Voyage of the Liberdade* are available in one paperback (New York: Collier Books, 1958), but are virtually unreadable. Sir Francis Chichester's *Gipsy Moth Circles the World* (New York: Coward-McCann, 1968) is believed by many to be a classic. I'd rate it a minor one, but it's certainly worth reading. My own favorite is a less celebrated but much better written little paperback by Robert Manry, a newspaper copyeditor: *Tinkerbelle* (New York: Dell, 1956) is the story of a single-handed trip across the Atlantic in a 13-foot, mostly homemade boat.

GUIDEBOOKS   There are numerous guides for sailors and other boaters, and they vary tremendously in quality.

Most owe their existence to the simple fact that sailors who are going someplace they haven't been before—the Caribbean, or maybe down the Intracoastal Waterway—need to know a lot about what lies before them, from water depths to hazards too recent to have been included on charts to information on where they can take on provisions. It's worthwhile borrowing or buying one of these guides just to see what they're like (and to fuel those deep-winter-evening fantasies). Examples include *Waterway Guide* (Annapolis), which is perhaps the best one, and *Boating Almanac* (Severna Park, Maryland), both of which are published annually in regional editions; and *Street's Cruising Guide to the Eastern Caribbean*, by Donald M. Street, Jr. (New York: W. W. Norton, 1980).

The *United States Coast Pilot* series (Washington: U.S. Department of Commerce) is published annually, with periodic corrections and updates in the weekly and local *Notices to Mariners*. It is essential for anyone who wants to bring a chart up to official snuff.

PERIODICALS AND ALMANACS   An expensive sport such as sailing supports a number of periodicals, as can be imagined. *Sail* magazine (34 Commercial Wharf, Boston, Massachusetts, 02110) is by definition dedicated to the sport, with stories on exciting passages, places to go, cruising, equipment, racing, and chartering—and, of course, those mouth-watering advertisements for sailboats. It's an attractive and useful magazine. But the one I like best is *Cruising World* (524 Thames Street, Newport, Rhode Island, 02840). It covers much the same territory as *Sail*, except it seems a little less slick, a little more down-home. I have the feeling that when the readers of *Sail* realize their lives would be better off if they had a portable table to protect their charts in the cockpit, or maybe a device to keep the halyards from slapping the mast all night, they go out and buy one, while the readers of *Cruising World* build one.

Cruising World contains, every now and again, a multi-color insert on heavy paper, marked for punching for a three-ring binder, called the "Cruising World Notebook." These inserts offer basic information on such topics as weather, aids to navigation, guides to boat insignia, knots and cordage, and emergency tactics. The sheets fit nicely into the notebook that every serious sailor starts to compile when he or she realizes there is no single source of information that meets all his or her personal needs.

Almanacs are big sailing items, with the added attraction (for their publishers) of the fact that they must be repurchased each year. And some are quite expensive. The *Nautical Almanac* (Washington and London: U.S. Naval Observatory and Her Majesty's Stationery Office) is a book full of numbers that you can use to figure out celestial observations, and little else. The *Eldridge Tide and Pilot Book* (Boston: Robert Eldridge White) contains information on tides, currents, lights, and weather on the east coast, along with rules of the road, astronomical data, first aid, and a lot of other material. *Reed's Nautical Almanac* (London: Thomas Reed Publications) does pretty much the same thing at pretty much twice the cost.

MARLINSPIKE   This is the pointed tool that is used by sailors to separate the strands of rope or wire while splicing, and it serves as the general term for all the mariner's dealings with rope, line, knots, and cordage. There are many books that explain nautical knots and splicing techniques; one of them is *The Art of Knots*, by Marc P. G. Berthier (Garden City, N.Y.: Doubleday, 1977), a nicely illustrated handbook.

WEATHER   The finest book I have seen on weather and the boater is named, appropriately, *Boating Weather* (New York: David McKay, 1978). Its authors, Sallie Townsend and Virginia Ericson, have turned out a splendidly useful book on everything the mariner needs to know about weather, including predicting it, obtaining and utilizing other people's predictions, and what to do about the weather that all sailors hope to avoid but that all know is unavoidable: storms. Even non-sailors would benefit from reading this one.

NAVIGATION   Not surprisingly, much of what is written about sailing is about navigation, of both the local and long-range varieties. And one man, Elbert S. Maloney, appears to be the major contributor to our current knowledge about getting where we want to go in boats. His edition of *Dutton's Navigation & Piloting* (Annapolis: Naval Institute Press, 1978) is a revision of a classic written in 1926 by a naval commander. This is close to a thousand pages of detailed instruction on navigation.

Maloney is also the editor/author of *Chapman: Piloting: Seamanship and Small Boat Handling* (New York: The Hearst Corporation, 1977), another thick book that many consider the absolute bible of boating. The first edition, written by Charles F. Chapman, came out in 1922, modestly referring to itself as "The Greatest Motor Boating Book Ever Published." If there is only one book a sailor could have, this would be the logical choice.

Two thinner but quite comprehensive books are *Practical Navigation for the Yachtsman*, revised edition (New York: W. W. Norton, 1972) by Frederick L. Devereux, Jr., and *Bowditch for Yachtsmen: Piloting* (New York: David McKay, 1976) by Nathaniel Bowditch. The latter is a standard book on piloting by the dean of American navigators, a mathematical wizard who lived from 1773 to 1838 and is best known for his *American Practical Navigator*, from which this book comes.

There are several books on the subject of celestial navigation. Many seem to be of the "Celestial Navigation for the Complete Nerd" variety, but one that I have read seems truly valuable—the aforementioned *Dutton's Navigation & Piloting*. A few contenders are *The Yachtsman's Guide to Celestial Navigation*, by Stafford Campbell (New York: Ziff-Davis, 1979); *Self-Taught Navigation*, by Robert Y. Kittredge (Flagstaff: Northland Press, 1970), and *Commonsense Celestial Navigation*, by Hewitt Schlereth (Chicago: Henry Regnery, 1975). An interesting and helpful book on the highlights and hardware of navigation, including celestial, is published by the U.S. Government: *A Navigation Compendium* (Washington: U.S. Government Printing Office, 1972). It is used in the Navy's officer candidate school and, it says, "within the fleet."

THE RULES   The Coast Guard publishes a book of *Navigation Rules*, both inland and international. These used to be called the Rules of the Road, and still are by everybody but the Coast Guard, which, being a government agency, must confuse things by calling the international part COLREGS (for International Regulations for Preventing Collisions at Sea). My copy of the rules is dated May 1, 1977, and when I tried to check in the summer of 1982 on the latest version I couldn't find anyone in the Coast Guard who seemed to know. If you'd like a copy of the Rules of the Road, I suggest you pester your local Coast Guard marine inspection office or, better yet, ask your congressperson for assistance.

Index

Index

Index

About the Author

Fred Powledge was born in North Carolina and has lived in Brooklyn for almost twenty years. He is the author of numerous nonfiction books, the most recent of which is *Water: The Nature, Uses, and Future of Our Most Precious and Abused Resource*, and has written extensively for magazines such as *The Nation*, *The New Yorker*, *Esquire*, *Life*, and *Harper's*. He teaches at the New School for Social Research in New York City.